# 外国语文论丛
董洪川 主编

# 英语教学法：理论与实践
English Language Teaching Methodology: Theory and Practice

刘玉梅 著

科学出版社
北京

## 内 容 简 介

本书分为八章。第一章为引言，主要说明了语言教学的本质及学习语言教学法的必要性。第二章回顾了主要的语言观和语言学习观，介绍了语言教学的新动向。第三章介绍了 11 种外语教学法，它们的主要特点和活动设计，增加了部分活动和解释。第四章介绍了 4 种外语教学的模式。第五、六章分别探讨了语音、词汇和句法的语言知识教学以及阅读、听力、口语和写作等语言技能教学，并配以较为丰富的例子。第七章分析了课程设计及课堂管理。第八章指出教师教育和发展的重要性及路径。

本书简明易懂，既可用作培养有志于从事外语教学的大学三、四年级学生的教科书，也可作为教师培训用书或参考书。

---

**图书在版编目（CIP）数据**

英语教学法：理论与实践 （English Language Teaching Methodology: Theory and Practice）/刘玉梅著. —北京：科学出版社，2020.6
（外国语文论丛 / 董洪川主编）
ISBN 978-7-03-063649-2

Ⅰ. ①英… Ⅱ. ①刘… Ⅲ. ①英语-教学法 Ⅳ. ①H319.3

中国版本图书馆 CIP 数据核字（2019）第 272192 号

---

责任编辑：杨　英 / 责任校对：贾伟娟
责任印制：徐晓晨 / 封面设计：蓝正设计

**科 学 出 版 社** 出版
北京东黄城根北街 16 号
邮政编码：100717
http://www.sciencep.com

**北京虎彩文化传播有限公司** 印刷
科学出版社发行　各地新华书店经销
*

2020 年 6 月第 一 版　　开本：720×1000　B5
2021 年 3 月第三次印刷　　印张：12
字数：240 000
**定价：98.00 元**
（如有印装质量问题，我社负责调换）

主　编：董洪川

副主编：王仁强

编　委：（按姓氏拼音顺序）

|  |  |  |  |
|---|---|---|---|
| 陈永国 | 程朝翔 | 冯亚琳 | 胡安江 |
| 黄国文 | 廖七一 | 罗选民 | 聂珍钊 |
| 宁　琦 | 彭青龙 | 乔国强 | 曲卫国 |
| 王初明 | 王克非 | 王文斌 | 王　寅 |
| 文　旭 | 向明友 | 熊沐清 | 许　钧 |
| 杨金才 | 姚继中 | 曾艳兵 | 查明建 |
| 张　涛 | 张旭春 | 祝朝伟 |  |

# 总　　序

四川外国语大学，简称"川外"（英文名为 Sichuan International Studies University，缩写为 SISU），位于歌乐山麓、嘉陵江畔，是我国设立的首批外语专业院校之一。古朴、幽深的歌乐山和清澈、灵动的嘉陵江涵养了川外独特的品格。学校在邓小平、刘伯承、贺龙等老一辈无产阶级革命家的关怀和指导下创建，从最初的中国人民解放军西南军政大学俄文训练团，到中国人民解放军第二高级步兵学校俄文大队，到西南人民革命大学俄文系、西南俄文专科学校，再到四川外语学院，最终于 2013 年更名为四川外国语大学，一路走来，70 年风雨兼程。学校从1979年开始招收硕士研究生，2013年被国务院学位委员会批准为博士学位授予单位。在 70 年的办学历程中，学校秉承"团结、勤奋、严谨、求实"的校训，发扬"守责、求实、开放、包容"的精神，精耕细作，砥砺前行，培养了一大批外语专业人才和复合型人才。他们活跃在各条战线上，为我国的外交事务、国际商贸、教学科研等各项建设事业做出了应有的贡献。

外国语言文学学科是学校的传统优势学科。几十年来，一代代学人素心焚膏、笃志穷远，默默耕耘于三尺讲台上，乐于清平，甘于奉献，在外国语言、外国文学与文化、翻译研究、中外文化交流等领域的人才培养和学术研究方面都取得了较为丰硕的成果。该学科不仅哺育了杨武能、蓝仁哲、刘小枫、黄长著、王初明、杜青钢、阮宗泽等众多有影响力的学者，还出版了《法汉大词典》《俄语教学词典》《英语教学词典》《加拿大百科全书》等大型工具书，在业界受到普遍欢迎。

近代历史发展证明，一个国家的兴衰与高等教育的发展休戚相关。现代性最早的种子在意大利萌芽，英国在 19 世纪成为"日不落帝国"，20 世纪的美国在科技领域领先全球……这些无不是其高等教育的发展使然。我国近代外语教育的奠基者张之洞在《劝学篇》中提出，"学术造人才，人才维国势"，将兴学育人与国势兴衰联系在一起。虽然他所主张的"中体西用"观点引发了不少争论，但其引进"西学"的历史意义是毋庸置疑的。然而，时过境迁，经过百余年的发展，特别是经过改革开放后 40 余年的努力，我国的外语教育取得了举世瞩目的成就。这不仅体现在日臻完备的人才培养体制上，还体现在外国语言研究、文学文化研究、翻译研究、教学研究等方方面面所取得的累累硕果上,更体现在外语教育为我国改革开放事业的蓬勃发展提供了大量的外语人才支撑上。因而,新时代的外语教育自然不再仅仅是张之洞所强调的引入"西学",而是具有了更深远、更重要的意义。

在新时代背景下,"一带一路"建设、"构建人类命运共同体"和"中华文化'走出去'"等国家战略对外语学科专业发展提出了新要求、新任务。外语教育不仅需要培养能倾听世界声音的外语专业人才,更需要培养能与世界对话、讲述中国故事、参与国际事务管理的复合型创新性人才。显然,新时代外语学科有了更重要的历史使命和责任担当。

基于上述认识,我们组织编写了"外国语文论丛"。这套丛书收录了外语学科文学、语言学、翻译学等多个领域的论著,不同作者在思维理念上虽然不可能完全一致,但是有一点似乎是共通的,那就是努力做到不尚空谈、不发虚辞。该丛书经过严格筛选程序,严把质量关,既注重对"外国语文"即外国语言、文学、文化及翻译的本体研究,也注重学科交叉或者界面研究、汉外对比、中外文化交流方面的成果,还特别注重对"讲好中国故事,传播好中国声音"具有启示意义的国外汉学研究、中国文化在国外传播研究方面的成果。

古人云:"君子务本,本立而道生。"我们希望通过出版这套丛书,推出学校外语学科的最新研究成果,积极推动我校外国语言文学学科的内涵建设,同时也为学界同仁提供一个相互学习、沟通交流的平台。

本丛书的出版得到了科学出版社的鼎力相助,也得到了学校外语学科广大教师的积极响应和支持,科学出版社的编辑和各位作者为此付出了艰辛的努力。尤其令我们感动的是,国内一批著名专家欣然同意担任本套丛书的编委,帮助我们把脉定向。在此,我谨向他们表示衷心的感谢和崇高的敬意!当然,由于时间仓促,也囿于我们自身的学识与水平,本丛书肯定还有诸多不足之处,恳请方家批评指正。

董洪川

2019 年深秋

于嘉陵江畔

# Preface

This is a revised version of the book initially published in 2007, made out of a series of scripts used in our teaching of English Language Teaching Methodology for junior and senior college students for years. In response to recent developments in language methodology, we make some changes and introduce a few new topics in some of the chapters. Our attempt is to provide a link between theory and practice: on the one hand, we explore insights into views of language and language learning, main teaching methods and approaches, and models of teaching processes, and on the other hand, we look at the theoretically supported practices of the teaching of the language system and language skills.

The book has been divided into eight chapters, each of which deals with a central theme but integrates with the other chapters as a whole. Chapter 1 discusses the nature of language teaching, the necessity of learning language teaching methodology, and the possibility of applying some of the key principles of cognitive linguistics into classroom language teaching. Chapter 2 provides an overview of the theories of language and language learning, which inform and underpin foreign language teaching. Chapter 3 outlines the main approaches in foreign language teaching, highlighting different guiding principles of teaching at different times. Chapter 4 introduces various models of the process of language teaching, such as the PPP model, the ESA model, the PPT model, and the TBL model. Chapter 5 and Chapter 6 attempt to relate the above-discussed principles and theories to the content of language teaching, which includes the teaching of the language system and language skills. The teaching of the language system deals with three subparts: the teaching of pronunciation, vocabulary, and grammar. The teaching of the language skills consists of four subparts: the teaching of reading, listening, speaking and writing. Chapter 7 focuses on lesson planning and classroom management. Chapter 8 examines, in brief, the significance of teacher education and development.

Each chapter deals with a central theme but integrates into a coherent, interdependent, and uniform whole as a book. It can be used as a coursebook for junior or senior college students who orient their interest in teaching English as a foreign language in their future career or used in training courses for novice and experienced teachers. It can also be a handbook for in-service teachers to conduct their self-learning through an evaluation of practices in reference to theories.

The revised edition of this book is funded by Sichuan International Studies University. In the course of editing this book, we owe credit to a considerable number of researchers for a variety of resources and materials from home and abroad. We would like to thank them all. Among those who deserve acknowledgment, we would also like to thank Professor Wang Yin,

Zhao Yongfeng, Wang Tianyi and Yang Ying who have offered comments and constructive suggestions in our revision.

Our thanks also go to our fellow colleagues and students, family and friends for their support in bringing this book to fruition.

Liu Yumei

Chongqing

March 2019

# Contents

总序

Preface

Chapter 1　Introduction ················································································ 1
　　1.1　The Nature of Language Teaching ······················································ 2
　　1.2　The Necessity of Learning Language Teaching Methodology ······· 4
　　1.3　New Trends in Language Teaching ···················································· 6
　　1.4　Overview of This Book ········································································· 8

Chapter 2　Views on Language and Language Learning ····················· 10
　　2.1　Views on Language ············································································ 11
　　2.2　Views on Language Learning ···························································· 16
　　2.3　Summary ······························································································ 20
　　2.4　Questions for Discussion ··································································· 21

Chapter 3　Major Methods and Approaches in FLT ······························ 23
　　3.1　The Grammar-Translation Method ··················································· 24
　　3.2　The Direct Method ·············································································· 26
　　3.3　The Audio-Lingual Approach ···························································· 27
　　3.4　The Silent Way ····················································································· 29
　　3.5　Suggestopedia ······················································································ 31
　　3.6　Community Language Teaching ······················································· 32
　　3.7　Total Physical Response ···································································· 34
　　3.8　The Cognitive Approach ···································································· 36
　　3.9　The Communicative Approach ························································· 37

| | 3.10 | Task-Based Language Teaching ··············································· 39 |
|---|---|---|
| | 3.11 | Learner-Centered Education ···················································· 40 |
| | 3.12 | Summary ··················································································· 41 |
| | 3.13 | Questions for Discussion ························································ 42 |

### Chapter 4  The Models of the Process of FLT ·································· 44
    4.1    The PPP Model ················································································ 46
    4.2    Harmer's ESA Model ······································································ 47
    4.3    Ur's PPT Model ················································································ 49
    4.4    Willis' TBL Model ··········································································· 51
    4.5    Summary ··························································································· 52
    4.6    Questions for Discussion ································································ 56

### Chapter 5  Teaching the Language System ····································· 57
    5.1    The Language System ······································································ 58
    5.2    Teaching Pronunciation ··································································· 61
    5.3    Teaching Vocabulary ······································································· 71
    5.4    Teaching Grammar ··········································································· 81
    5.5    Summary ··························································································· 89
    5.6    Questions for Discussion ································································ 89

### Chapter 6  Teaching Language Skills ············································· 91
    6.1    Reading ······························································································ 92
    6.2    Listening ··························································································· 109
    6.3    Speaking ··························································································· 124
    6.4    Writing ······························································································ 132

### Chapter 7  Lesson Planning and Classroom Management ············ 141
    7.1    Lesson Planning ··············································································· 142
    7.2    Classroom Management ·································································· 157

7.3　Questions for Discussion ................................................................ 164

Chapter 8　Teacher Education and Development ................................ 166

References ................................................................................................ 171

# Chapter 1
## Introduction

> *What distinguishes the human brain is the variety of more specialized activities it is capable of learning. The preeminent example is language.*
>
> *(Geschwind, 1979: 192)*

> *...in some for or another it (language) so dominates our social and cognitive activity that it would be difficult to imagine what life would be without it.*
>
> *(Harley, 2001:1)*

The first chapter of the book inquires into the nature of language teaching, the necessity of learning language teaching methodology and new trends in it. It provides a conceptual setting for the discussions in the succeeding chapters.

## 1.1 The Nature of Language Teaching

Teaching is an art as well as a science, which is also true to language teaching. Like all sciences, language teaching has a set of underlying principles upon which it is based. However, unlike such sciences as mathematics, physics, and chemistry which rely more on objectivity, language teaching, more like psychology and sociology, must rely on objectivity as well as subjectivity in order to tap into professional research and education, observe class instructions, synthesize individual experience and others' experiences, and formulate its principles in instructional practices. In return, these guiding principles, through constant practical verification in real instructional practices, bring their adaptation and adjustment to accomplishment.

Through all ages, there have been different parlance about the nature of language teaching. For instance, Stern (1983) defines language teaching as the activities which are intended to bring about language learning. Widdowson (1990) investigates the nature of language teaching as a principled professional activity. In his investigation, he explores the significance of the interdependence of theory and practice. One the one hand, language teaching can be seen as a principled problem-solving activity. It is a kind of operational research which works out solutions to its own local problems in instructional practices. On the other hand, teaching theories may serve as guiding principles in real instructional practices. Only within the domain of application, namely, through the immediate activity of teaching, can the interdependent relationship between theory and practice, ideas and their actualization be realized. Therefore, in matching up theories with practices, experimentation and meditation are at least involved. Still, he sees teaching as a research activity which involves principled techniques in learning and experiment so as to enquire into the relationship between theory and practice. Teaching provides development not only for learners but also for teachers, and thus, in the end, this interactive development promotes the learning to a higher degree. Based on this view, he proposes a model of mediation of language teaching.

Ur (1996) understands language teaching as what is intended to result in personal learning for students. Based on his observation, he proposes the enriched model which attaches importance not only to concrete experience from real teaching practice but also to various input from external sources, such as other people's observation, professional research, theorizing, and other people's experiments. "The contexts of language teaching, like the more general social contexts within which they are located, are continually changing, continually challenging habitual ways of thinking and patterns of past certainty. Unless there is a corresponding process of critical appraisal, there can be no adaptation, no adjustment to change" (Widdowson, 1990).

## 1.2  The Necessity of Learning Language Teaching Methodology

There always seems to be an argument that without any knowledge of theories or principles of teaching, one might as well be able to teach a language based on his or her own experience or intuitive sense of direction. However, teaching based only on personal experience and minimal practical skills will not go too far. Widdowson (1990) comments that "teachers tend to be referred as if they were factory workers to be provided with minimal practical skills and required to pick up on the job whatever extra expertise is necessary to keep the production line going." To reach standards of professionalism depends much on "a continual process of self-education through an evaluation of practice in reference to theory" (Widdowson, 1990).

One who knows a language well does not necessarily mean that he or she can teach that language well. We find that teaching and learning are bi-directionally interacting; teaching theory and teaching practice are mutually enhancing. On the one hand, experience, experimentation, and observation in real-time teaching activities help to shape language teaching theories. On the other hand, these theories will, in reverse, act on instructional practice. Besides, interdisciplinary knowledge (e.g., psychology, sociology, pedagogy, management science) assists in language teaching.

In a real teaching context of a language, there has always been tension between theory and practice. Therefore, regardless of the common senses which teaching requires, a lot more factors have to be taken into account so as to facilitate good teaching: the nature of the language to be taught, teaching content and its sequence to be carried out in teaching practice, individual differences, the interpersonal relationships that exist between the teacher and the student or the student and other students or even students, the learning environment, the instruction setting, the management of the equipment, the time available for instruction, assessment, the teaching results, etc.

In consideration of the variety and complexity of all those factors in teaching practice, one can hardly do a better job without resorting to some guiding principles. Contrarily, without retrospection of and reflection on the experiences in real instructional practices, one cannot bring the guiding principles into full play.

It seems that the development of professional competence probably is the most important and difficult part of training a good language teacher from whom adequate qualifications are demanded, such as a good mastery of that language, know-how of language theories and learning theories, specific skills, strategies and ability, a general range of interdisciplinary knowledge, etc.

Therefore, teacher training and education sound as equally important as students' development, as the former imposes a direct impact on the latter and vice versa. This is what the making of a successful language teacher counts.

## 1.3 New Trends in Language Teaching

Cognitive linguistics is a relatively new enterprise whose basic tenets are becoming influential in the area of the second language or foreign language teaching. In recent years, a few cognitive linguists and language educators have converged to explore the application of the key concepts and principles of cognitive linguistics to the teaching and learning of foreign languages. In 2001, there were two volumes edited by Martin Pütz, Susanne Niemeier, and René Dirven, addressing a number of important topics in the theory, acquisition, and pedagogy from the perspective of cognitive linguistics: *Applied Cognitive Linguistics I: Theory and Language Acquisition* and *Applied Cognitive Linguistics II: Language Pedagogy*. In 2008, Frank Boers and Seth Lindstromberg published a volume of *Cognitive Linguistic Approaches to Teaching Vocabulary and Phraseology*, Peter Robinson and Nick Ellis (1999) wrote *Handbook of Cognitive Linguistics and Second Language Acquisition*,

Sabine De Knop and Teun De Rycker brought out *Cognitive Approaches to Pedagogical Grammar: A Volume in Honour of* René Dirven. In 2009, there were two monographs: *Cognitive Linguistics and Language Teaching* by Randal Holme, and *Applying Cognitive Linguistics to Second Language Learning and Teaching* by Jeannette Littlemore. Teresa Cadierno, Wind Eskildsen edited a volume of *Usage-Based Perspectives on Second Language Learning* in 2015. In 2016, Franka Kermer published *A Cognitive Grammar Approach to Teaching Tense and Aspect in the L2 Context*.

Although they did not make any claims to methodological novelty, they ventured to seek answers to some of the traditional problems concerning the nature of the meaning of language and focus on the interaction between language, communication, cognition, and acquisition in general.

The cognitive venture to language teaching is mostly based on the following tenets of cognitive linguistics.

1) Language is part of a cognitive system that comprises perception, emotions, categorization, abstract processes, and reasoning (Dirven and Verspoor, 1998).

2) Language is usage-based in that it depends on and itself influences conceptualization, which is controlled by our experiences of ourselves, the external world and our relation to that world (Pütz, Niemeier, and Dirven, 2001a).

3) Language units are subject to categorization, which commonly gives rise to prototype-based networks; much of it critically involves metaphor and metonymy.

Based on the above assumption, the above volumes and monographs endeavor to explore the basic concepts: prototype, categorization, construal, attention, metaphor, metonymy, embodiment, conceptualization, construction, image schema, cognitive model, blending space, et al., and to look at how they relate to second or foreign language teaching and learning. As Littlemore (2009: 4) claims, "some of these concepts give rise to possible new ways of teaching languages, whereas others provide further support for existing methodologies."

## 1.4 Overview of This Book

It is too huge a task to cover all principles and theories of language teaching and learning in one book. Moreover, it is all the more impossible to note down all the practical experiences of each teaching case. The overall aim of this book is to provide some theories and practices in brief, which may shed light on our understanding of theory and practice in language teaching and learning.

The contents of this book have been organized as follows. Chapter 1 discusses the nature of language teaching and the necessity of learning language teaching methodology. Chapter 2 provides an overview of the theories of language and language learning which inform and underpin foreign language teaching. Chapter 3 outlines the main approaches in foreign language teaching, highlighting different guiding principles of teaching at different times. Chapter 4 introduces different models of the language teaching process. Chapter 5 and Chapter 6 attempt to relate the above-discussed principles and theories to the content of language teaching, including the teaching of the language system and language skills. Chapter 7 focuses on lesson planning and classroom management. Chapter 8 examines the significance of teacher education and development.

# Chapter 2

## Views on Language and Language Learning

*Language is a process of free creation; its laws and principles are fixed, but the manner in which the principles of generation are used is free and infinitely varied. Even the interpretation and use of words involves a process of free creation.*

*(Noam Chomsky, 1970: 344 )*

*Language offers a window into cognitive function, providing insights into the nature, structure and organization of thoughts and ideas. ... is assumed to reflect certain fundamental properties and design features of the human mind.*

*(Evans and Green, 2006: 5)*

This chapter is to provide an overview of the theories of language and language learning which inform and underpin foreign language teaching.

When we discuss language teaching and learning, first, we have to answer "What is language?" How we understand language may be the basis for syllabus design, teaching methods used in instructional practices, teaching procedures in the classroom, and even the techniques used in the class. Based on different views on language, teaching methodologies may vary to some degree.

## 2.1 Views on Language

"What is language?" may at first sound like a simple question that does not deserve effort to answer, for we always take it for granted that it should be a part of life as walking and eating. Modern linguists have defined language in various ways with each having its special emphasis and limitations. Generally, language involves at least three activities: neural activity in the brain, muscular activity in the human body, and social activity that engages individuals interacting with one another and with the written language (胡壮麟和姜望琪, 2002).

People take different views on the study of language from different angles. A summary made by Richards & Rodgers (1986) shows that the structural view is more influential than the functional view and the interactional view. In addition to the above three views, there are also the instrumental view, the innate view, and the experiential cognitive view. Wang Yin (王寅, 2005) explains in brief in his *Explorations on Cognitive Linguistics* (《认知语言学探索》)how these views are influenced by other disciplines and in turn, influences the formation and development of language teaching methodology. The following part explains the axioms and theoretical framework that may motivate a particular teaching method.

### 2.1.1　The Instrumental View

Before the 19$^{th}$ century, people took a prescriptive study of language which prescribed what should be done and should not be done in a language. The language was seen as static and descriptive. In the 19$^{th}$ century, people took a historical-comparative study of language. This view of language was embodied in the grammar-translation method (in 3.1), which historically used in teaching Greek and to gain access to classical literature.

### 2.1.2　The Structural View

The structural view takes a rigid descriptive approach in linguistic study, which has its influence from some other disciplines such as analytic philosophy, behaviorism. It sees language as a system of structurally related elements for the transmission of meaning. A linguistic system is made up of various subsystems: phonological, morphological, lexical, and syntactical. Therefore, the target of language learning is seen to be the mastery of elements of this system (Richards & Rodgers, 1986).

Based on this view of language, some of the language learning approaches are generated, e. g., the audiolingual approach (in 3.3) (Richards & Rodgers, 1986). Some contemporary methods which embody this view of language are the silent way (in 3.4) and total physical response (in 3.7) (Rodgers, 2001; Nunan, 2004).

## 2.1.3 The Functional View

The communicative or functional view of language takes a communicative and functional approach in linguistic studies, which is influenced by other disciplines such as sociology and behaviorism. It views language as a vehicle for the expression of functional meaning. The semantic and communicative dimensions of language are more emphasized than the grammatical characteristics, although these are also included (Richards & Rodgers, 1986). This view of language is embodied in the language learning approach, such as the communicative approach or functional-notional approach (in 3.9) which later leads to the emergence of task-based language teaching (in 3.10) and learner-centered education (in 3.11) (Nunan, 2004).

## 2.1.4 The Interactional view

The interactional view of language sees language primarily as the means for establishing and maintaining interpersonal relationships and for performing social transactions between individuals. Language teaching content may be specified and organized by patterns of exchange and interaction or may be left unspecified, to be shaped by the inclinations of learners as interaction. Therefore, the target of language learning in this view is learning to initiate and maintain conversations with other people. This view probably facilitates the development of the communicative approach (Richards & Rodgers, 1986).

## 2.1.5 The Innatist View

Under the influence of Descartesian philosophy, formalism, and mentalism, language is generally seen as "a mirror of the mind" (Chomsky, 1975). The innate view of language emphasizes that human beings, equipped genetically with Language Acquisition Device (LAD), are capable of language learning provided with adequate input. LAD produces internalized languages or I-languages with which a person can generate new expressions over an unbounded range and engage in the "creative use of language" (Smith, 1999). Therefore, language is believed to be creative, stimulus-free and rule-governed behavior. This view brings about the emergence of the cognitive approach, also known as cognitive code-learning theory (in 3.8).

## 2.1.6 The Experiential Cognitive View

The experiential cognitive perspective, under the influence of embodied philosophy and mental-constructivism, holds that language is part of a cognitive system that comprises perception, emotions, categorization, abstract processes, and reasoning. All these cognitive abilities interact with language and are influenced by language (Dirven & Verspoor, 1998). Under the influence of this view, the cognitive teaching approach is underway (王寅, 2005). As Dirven, Niemeier & Pütz (2001: xi) pointed out, "in its view of language as being based on and rooted in cognition, CL (Cognitive Linguistics) can only accept that both processes-unconscious acquisition and awareness in learning—go hand in hand and are always both present in language instruction scenarios, albeit in widely varying degrees."

Each view has its own focuses. To some degree, these views of language have complementarily facilitated our understanding of the nature of language. The instrumental view only focuses on the instrumental function of language. The structural view limits a language to a closed system with its structural rules and vocabulary. The functional view stresses the need to know how to use the rules and vocabulary for real communication. The interactional view pays more attention to the social functions of the language used in communicative contexts. The innate view takes grammar back in fashion but in a different sense. And the experiential cognitive view sees language as part of a human cognitive system. The above views of language provide the axioms and theoretical framework that may motivate particular teaching methods and approaches, such as the audio-lingualism, the communicative approach, the task-based approach, the cognitive approach, etc. But in themselves, they are incomplete and used to be complemented by theories of language learning (Richards & Rodgers, 1986). In 2.2, we will examine views on language learning.

## 2.2　Views on Language Learning

A theory of language learning is an account of the central processes (e.g., psycholinguistic and cognitive processes) involved in language learning and the conditions that need to be met for these processes to take place and promote successful language learning. That means theories of language learning explain what happens when learning actually takes place. There are different theories of language learning in the literature. For instance, Richards and Rodgers (1986) assume that language learning theories can be broadly divided into process-oriented theories and condition-oriented theories.

A process-oriented language learning theory is a theory built on describing learning processes, how the mind processes new information, such as habit-formation, induction, making inferences, hypothesis-testing, generalization.

A condition-oriented language learning theory places stress upon the human and physical context in which language learning takes place. These factors have to be taken into consideration: the number of students, what kind of input learners receive, and the learning atmosphere.

However, according to Krashen (1981), learning is a conscious process by which the formal study of language rules is carried out. From the perspective of psychology, language learning can generally be seen in three types: behaviorist theory, cognitive theory, and constructivist theory.

## 2.2.1 A Behaviorist View of Language Learning

The primary theorists involved with behaviorism are J.Watson, E. Thorndike, and B. F. Skinner. Behaviorism is also called connectionist theory. Hence, connectionism puts its focus on behavioral psychology (Thorndike, 1932). Based on observable changes in behavior, it uses a stimulus-response model to describe and explain learning behaviors. Learning is seen to take place through the process of habit formation. Visually, the logic looks like this in Figure 2-1.

$$S—r—s—R$$

**Figure 2-1　Stimulus-Response Theory**

The behaviorist theory of language learning is derived from general behavioristic learning theory. The idea of this theory is that language is a form of behavior. It can be developed in much the same manner as other skills: through a process of habit formation in which habits are formed by constant imitation and reinforced by continuous repetition during which mistakes are immediately corrected.

The behaviorist theory of language learning and the structural theory of language provide a theoretical framework for the emergence of the audiolingual approach, which is characterized by a variety of drill-based techniques and exercises.

## 2.2.2 An Innatist or Mentalist View of Language Learning

Cognitivism is proposed as a strong objection to the inadequate representation of the learning process viewed by behaviorism. It focuses on an unobservable change in mental knowledge. In opposition to the ideas of behaviorism, some learning processes are considered unique to human beings and the cognitive processes, as the focus of study, exert influence on learning. Learning is not mechanical imitation but involves the formation of mental associations that are not necessarily reflected in overt behavior changes.

Wertheimer (1923) and Bruner (1987), advocates of Gestalt Psychology, see learning as cognitive in nature, which includes the memory system as an active processor of information. For Chomsky (1975), cognitive theories of learning should focus on the mind, which is assumed to be equipped with LAD as an innate ability that contains principles that are universal to all human languages. This innate ability is redefined as Universal Grammar (UG) by Chomsky. What guides the acquisition of learning is this innate system rather than conditioning. Therefore, with the processing of UG, children can generate new expressions and engage in the creative use of language. According to Chomsky, language is not a form of behavior, it is an intricate rule-based system and a large part of language acquisition is the learning of this system.

## 2.2.3 A Constructivist View of Language Learning

The concept of constructivism can trace back to the ancient times of Socrates and Lao Tzu (Pritchard & Woollard, 2010). In objection to the objectivist view of knowledge transmission, constructivism embodies an epistemological alternative which places stress upon the active role of learner who constructs their knowledge based on their past experiences. The most prominent representatives of constructivism are John Dewey, Jean Piaget, Lev Vygotsky, and Jerome Bruner. According to Dewey's (1997) philosophy of education, learning should be grounded in real experiences and engaged in creativity and collaboration. Piaget (1972) proposes a dynamic process of learning. In this view, learning is regarded as a self-directed process of constructing our understanding of the world in which we engage.

It is Vygotsky (1978, 1986) who has introduced the social aspect of learning into constructivism. Learning is perceived rather as a process of knowledge construction than passive absorption, which is based upon not only personal experiences but also socio-cultural factors with an emphasis on the role of others and social interaction in the process of constructing knowledge and understanding. Bruner (1973) also considers learning as an active process in which learners construct new ideas and concepts by connecting to their current and pre-existing knowledge. Learners are usually involved in the active construction of conceptual structures through reflection and abstraction, just like a journey of discovery. The principles of that constructivism give rise to some learning approaches such as learner-centered education, cooperative learning, experiential learning, etc.

## 2.3 Summary

The affinities of language theories and language learning theories have generated different teaching methodologies. For instance, the linking of structuralism to behaviorist theory produces the audiolingual approach (in 3.3) which further spawns other alternatives such as the silent way (in 3.4); suggestopedia (in 3.5); community language learning (in 3.6); total physical response (in 3.7) (Rodgers, 2001). The linking of the functional view of language to cognitive theory generates the communicative approach (in 3.9) which spawns off-shoots such as task-based language teaching (in 3.10); learner-centered education (in 3.11) (Rodgers, 2001; Nunan, 1988). We will not discuss how to apply the tenets of cognitive linguistics to second or foreign language teaching.

No matter what theory of language or what theory of language learning is, as Richards and Rodgers (1986) suggest, "teachers may develop their own teaching procedures, informed by a particular view of language and a particular theory of language learning. They may constantly revise, vary, and modify teaching and learning procedures on the basis of the performance of the learners and their reactions to instructional practice. A group of teachers holding a similar belief about language and language learning may each implement these principles in different ways".

## 2.4 Questions for Discussion

1) What is language? In what sense language is viewed as a system, vocal, and symbolic? Do you agree with the belief that language is arbitrary?

2) In this chapter, we discussed different views of language and views of language learning. How do these views of language and language learning

differ from each other?

3) How are language teaching approaches motivated by the theory of language and theory of language learning?

4) Do you think that all theories of language or theories of language learning will necessarily lead to language teaching approaches? Explain your view with reasons.

# Chapter 3
# Major Methods and Approaches in FLT

*They may constantly revise, vary, and modify teaching/ learning procedures on the basis of the performance of the learners and their reactions to instructional practice.*

*( Richards & Rodgers 1986:19 )*

*Learning is finding out what you already know; Doing is demonstrating that you know it; Teaching is reminding others that they know it as well as you do. We are all learners, doers, and teachers.*

*(Bach, 1977: 31)*

Foreign Language Teaching (FLT) is a science, and like all sciences, it has a set of underlying principles upon which it is based. In order to teach English effectively, an English as a Foreign Language (EFL) teacher must subscribe to one or more of the current approaches to teach English as a foreign language and incorporate its language-learning strategies and techniques into his or her lessons.

To review all language teaching methods or approaches could be a big undertaking. So we can try to give a brief review of the major ones which are placed in a sequence based on the views of language and language learning theory. Some of them you may feel very familiar with in your own classroom learning or teaching history. Hopefully, you may have a brief outline of the evolution of ideas that have marked the emergence of newer and different approaches to language teaching.

## 3.1 The Grammar-Translation Method

The grammar-translation method, which is also called the "traditional method", the "old method", or the "classical method", is the byproduct of the historical-comparative study of language. Language is seen as an instrument for the appreciation of classical literature. This approach was historically used in teaching Greek and Latin which were known as "dead languages" for the purpose of gaining access to classical literature. The approach was gradually extended to modern language teaching. On the whole, the method characterizes highly structured classwork with the teacher controlling all activities.

**Major Activities:**

1) asking questions after a passage reading.

2) translating literary passages from one language to another.

3) memorizing grammar rules.

4) memorizing native-language equivalents of the target language vocabulary.

**Major Characteristics**

1) Teaching in the mother tongue of the students, with little active use of the target language.

2) Teaching vocabulary in the form of isolated word lists with equivalents of the target language.

3) Elaborate explanations of grammar with example sentences.

4) Providing the rules for putting words together in grammar instruction; focusing on the form and inflection of words.

5) Facilitating difficult texts reading at the beginning of study for exercises in grammatical analysis with little attention to the content of texts.

6) Practice in translating disconnected sentences from the target language into the mother tongue, and vice versa.

7) Little or no attention to pronunciation.

## 3.2 The Direct Method

The direct method develops initially as a reaction to the grammar-translation approach. The emergence of the "direct method" is based on the naturalistic language learning principles developing from the observation of child language learning. This method attempts to restrict the use of the mother tongue and use more target language in oral communication. It advocates that all foreign language teaching should perform in the target language only, with no translation and an emphasis on linking meaning to the language being learned. Under such circumstances, more stress is placed on spontaneous use of the language and the ability to "think" in the target language. The method became very popular during the first quarter of the 20th century and was especially quite successful in private language schools in European countries. However, it is difficult to implement in public educational institutions for several reasons, such as the realities of the classroom, lack of theoretical knowledge in applied linguistics, etc.

**Major Activities**

1) Initial preparation by a drill.

2) Habit-forming by practicing similar drills.

3) Accuracy achieved from correcting mistakes.

**Major Characteristics**

1) Classroom instruction is carried out only in the target language.

2) Concrete new material is first presented orally with actions or pictures. Abstract material is taught by association of ideas.

3) The preferred type of exercise is a series of question-and-answer exchanges in the target language.

4) Grammar is taught inductively—rules are generalized from the practice and experience with the target language.

5) Only everyday vocabulary and sentences are taught.

## 3.3 The Audio-Lingual Approach

The audio-lingual approach is based on the structural view of language and the behavioral theory of learning. This approach originating as the army method in the United States, evolves a parallel approach of situational language teaching in European countries.

The army method coincided with World War II when the United States became aware that it needed people to learn foreign languages very quickly as part of its overall military operations in the world. Thus this method was developed to build conversational competence in a variety of languages through very intensive language courses that focused on aural/oral skills.

In combination with some new ideas about language from the disciplines of descriptive linguistics and language learning from behavioral psychology, the army method went on to become what is known as the audiolingual approach. Through this approach, which was also called a modified direct method, adapted many of the principles and procedures of the direct method, it added the concepts of teaching "linguistic patterns" in combination with "habit-forming". It placed stress on mastering the elements or building blocks of the language and learning the rules by which these elements are combined.

The audiolingual approach promoted a variety of alternative approaches such as the silent way (in 3.4), suggestopedia (in 3.5), community language learning (in 3.6), and total physical response (in 3.7) (Rodgers, 2001).

**Major Characteristics**

1) Priority is given to spoken rather than written language and new material is presented in the form of a dialogue.

2) Language learning is assumed to be a matter of habit-forming through imitation, memorization, and reinforcement.

3) Structures are sequenced and taught one at a time. Structural patterns are taught by repetitive drills.

4) Grammar is taught inductively and little or no grammatical

explanations are provided.

5) Communicative skills are sequenced: listening, speaking, reading and writing are developed in order.

6) Aural-oral training is needed to provide the foundation for the development of other skills.

7) Vocabulary is strictly limited in a linguistic and cultural context.

8) Great importance is given to precise native-like pronunciation.

9) The teacher is permitted to use the mother tongue, which may discourage the students.

10) Successful responses are reinforced; great care is taken to help learners to correct errors immediately.

11) There is a tendency to disregard content and meaning.

## 3.4 The Silent Way

It was Caleb Gattegno who founded "the silent way" as a method for language learning in the early 1970s and viewed language itself as "a substitute for experience, so experience is what gives meaning to language" (Gattegno, 1972). It shared many of the same essential learning theories and educational philosophies that viewed learning as a "problem-solving, creative, discovering activity" (Richards & Rodgers, 1986) to be engaged in by the students both independently and as a group. In this learning activity, the learner was a principal actor rather than a bench-bound listener, and the teacher stayed "out of the way" in the process of learning as much as possible. This idea is best represented in the words of Benjamin Franklin: (quoted in Richards & Rodgers, 1986).

*Tell me and I forget,*
*Teach me and I remember,*
*Involve me and I learn.*

The silent way was also well-known for the colored rods of varying length and color-coded word charts depicting pronunciation values, vocabulary and grammatical paradigms. These visual devices were used as associative mediators for student learning and recall (Richards & Rodgers, 1986). It was probably the first kind to concentrate on cognitive principles in language learning.

Some of Caleb Gattegno's basic theories were that "teaching should be subordinated to learning" and "the teacher works with the student; the student works on the language" (Gattegno, 1972). As the term suggested, the teacher, as a facilitator and stimulator, typically stayed "silent" most of the time.

**Major Characteristics**

1) Tokens and charts are used as central elements in teaching.

2) Students are encouraged to grasp the "spirit" of the language, not just its component forms.

3) Lessons are sequenced and taught one at a time according to grammatical complexity.

4) A sentence is the basic unit of teaching.

5) The structural patterns of the target language are presented and the grammar rules are learned inductively.

6) The functional vocabulary, such as everyday items of the target language, is learned first.

7) Learners play the role of a teacher, a student, part of a supporting system, a problem solver, and an evaluator.

## 3.5 Suggestopedia

Suggestopedia is a language learning method developed by the Bulgarian psychologist Georgi Lozanov in the late 1970s. It is formulated on the belief that students naturally set up psychological barriers to learning. The barriers are based on the fears that they are unable to perform and are thus limited in terms of their ability to learn. According to Lozanov, learners might have been using only 5 to 10 percent of their mental capacity, and if given "optimal" conditions for learning, the brain could process and retain much more material. Based on psychological research on extrasensory perception, Lozanov began to develop a language learning method that finally became known as "suggestopedia".

**Major Characteristics**

1) Soft music is used during the learning process to create relaxed concentration that facilitates the intake and retention of vast quantities of material.

2) Complete control and authority are given to the teacher to create a situation in which the learners are most suggestible.

3) A learner's mental stage is crucial to success. Students are encouraged to maintain a pseudo-passive state.

4) Listening practice takes place on the first day of learning a new unit.

5) A four-hour language class consists of three distinct parts: oral review, presentation of and discussion on new material, and séance or concert session.

## 3.6　Community Language Teaching

Community Language Learning (CLL) was developed by Charles Curran and his associates in the United States in the 1970s. It applied counseling techniques to language teaching. In addition to the structuralist positions on the nature of language which was developed to be an alternative theory of language known as "language as a social process," it was influenced by the humanistic pedagogy and sometimes cited as an example of a "humanistic approach". In this method, the learner is not thought of as a student but as a client. The instructors of the target language are trained in counseling skills as language counselors.

CLL (Curran, 1976a/1976b) proposes a "whole-person" learning which takes place in a communicative situation, the process of which is divided into five stages. In stage one, the learner entirely depends on the instructor for linguistic content and repeats what the teacher utters in the target language and "overhears" the exchanges between others. After the instructor reflects the learner in the target language, it comes to stage two. The learner begins to establish his or her self-affirmation and independence by presenting his or her ideas in simple languages in the target language. In stage three, the learner begins to understand others directly and speaks to the group in the target language. In stage four, the learner speaks freely and complexly in the foreign language and the instructor directly corrects grammatical errors and mispronunciations. Stage five is called the independent stage. The instructor and the learner exchange freely and independently, refining his or her understanding of idiomatic use of the target language (Richards & Rodgers, 1986).

### Major Characteristics

1) The counselor-client relationship is central to teaching.

2) Language is used to express one's thoughts.

3) Anxiety is reduced in the learning experience.

4) Stress is placed on group work, reflection, and observation.

5) Cognitive and affective factors are taken into great consideration.

## 3.7 Total Physical Response

Under the influence of developmental psychology, learning theory and humanistic pedagogy and language theories, Total Physical Response (TPR) was developed by James Asher in the 1970s (Asher, 1979). It is a language teaching method built around the coordination of speech and action, attempting to teach language through physical or motor activities (Richards & Rodgers, 1986).

TPR is linked to the insight into the "trace theory" of memory in psychology, which is stimulated and increased when it is closely associated with motor activity. Based on observation of how children acquire their mother tongue, this method also assumes that the learning process involves a substantial amount of listening and comprehension in combination with various "physical responses" before learners begin to use the language orally. As effective factors were concerned, it also calls for a comfortable, dynamic and stress-free learning environment in which physical activities are used.

This method is generally considered as a highly effective method at beginning levels, especially in the instruction of young learners.

**Major Characteristics**

1) Developing comprehension skills is emphasized before the learner is taught to speak.

2) Imperatives are the main structures to communicate information.

3) Meaning rather than form is emphasized in teaching.

4) Games are often used in teaching to create a comfortable, dynamic and stress-free learning environment.

The usual format of a TPR lesson goes as follows:

Step 1 The teacher says the command as he himself performs the action.

Step 2 The teacher says the command as both the teacher and the students then perform the action.

Step 3 The teacher says the command, but only students perform the action.

Step 4 The teacher tells one student at a time to perform actions.

Step 5 The roles of teacher and student are reversed. Students give commands to the teacher and other students.

Step 6 The teacher and student allow for command expansion or produce new sentences.

## 3.8  The Cognitive Approach

In addition to the challenge of cognitive psychology to language learning, another challenge to the structuralism was proposed by N. Chomsky in the 1950s, known as transformational-generative grammar. These concepts severely challenged the idea that language learning was all about imitation, reinforcement, and habit-formation. On the one hand, they argued that language was not a form of behavior. The famous argument was, "if all language is a learned behavior, how can a child produce a sentence that has never been said by others before?" To them, the language was an intricate rule-based system and a large part of language acquisition was the learning of this system. On the other hand, they placed emphasis on an active mental process in which rules were formed rather than a process of habit formation in language learning.

Under the influence of language theory and learning theory, the cognitive approach was developed in the 1960s, also known as cognitive code learning. Its representative advocates were cognitive psychologists and applied linguists, J. B. Carroll and K. Chastain. They argued that human cognition could be used to process and discover the rules of the target language. It was sometimes regarded as grammar back in fashion as what grammar-translation method did in the 19th century. (Nunan, 2004) Classroom activities were designed to encourage learners to work out grammar rules for themselves through deductive reasoning.

**Major Characteristics**

1) Language learning is the acquisition of rules, not habit formation.

2) Grammar is emphasized and taught deductively.

3) Reading and writing are as important as listening and speaking.

4) Learning is an active mental process.

5) Human cognition is stressed in the process of learning.

## 3.9 The Communicative Approach

The communicative approach, also known as the notional approach, or semantic-notional approach, or the communicative language teaching, was developed by British applied linguists as a challenge to structure-based approaches such as the audiolingual approach. This approach was generally patterned upon multidisciplinary perspectives, such as the functional view of language advocated by J. Firth and M. A. K. Halliday, American sociolinguistic work represented by D. Hymes and W. Labov, and philosophical view of languages such as speech act theory and indirect speech act theory headed by J. Austin and J. Searle (Richards & Rodgers, 1986). This approach emphasized the functional and communicative potential of language and argued that language teaching should focus on communicative proficiency rather than on mere mastery of structures. Therefore, it did a lot to expand on the goal of creating "communicative competence" compared with earlier methods, which though professed the same objective, failed to do so. Teaching students how to use the language was considered to be as important as learning the language itself.

The communicative approach "has spawned a number of off-shoots that share the same basic set of principles, but which spell out philosophical details or envision instructional practices in somewhat diverse ways," such as "The natural approach, cooperative language learning, content-based teaching, and task-based teaching" (Rodgers, 2001). Nunan (1989) points out that this approach "has been realized methodologically by task-based language teaching" (in 3.10) and "also reinforced another trend: learner-centered education" (3.11).

**Major Characteristics**

1) Learners learn a language by using it to communicate.

2) Authentic and meaningful communication should be the goal of classroom activities.

3) Fluency is an important dimension of communication.

4) Communication involves the integration of different language skills.

5) Learning is a process of creative construction and involves trial and error (Rodgers, 2001).

## 3.10　Task-Based Language Teaching

Task-based approach to teaching language is a recent view which is based on the findings of linguists and psychologists. This approach is against traditional approaches, such as the audiolingual approach of language teaching represented by the PPP (Presentation, Practice, Production) models. It can be seen as a significant further evolution of communicative language teaching, both in terms of views of language in use and the development of classroom methodology (McDonough & Shaw, 2004). It is formalized by J. Willis (1996), who defines tasks as activities where "the target language is used by the learner for a communicative purpose…in order to achieve an outcome."

Traditionally language learning has been regarded as a process of mastering a succession of structures, each one building on the one before, such as from sounds to words, and from words to sentences. Task-based teaching views learning as a set of communicative tasks in which communication and interaction are as important as accuracy and fluency.

Task-based syllabus is the cornerstone of the task-based teaching approach. It is usually organized in terms of some different kinds of tasks rather than in terms of grammar or vocabulary. The learners are expected to carry out the outside class tasks in the target language in class.

Task-based teaching approach falls into three stages: the pre-task stage, the "task cycle" and the "language focus" stage which will be explained explicitly in 4.4.

**Major Characteristics**

1) Language is used for a genuine purpose.

2) Language form should be considered in general rather than in a single form.

3) The four language skills are integrated into doing tasks.

## 3.11　Learner-Centered Education

Learner-centered education is a contrary term to teacher-centered education in which teaching and learning are considered as an "instructional paradigm" with the teacher as a dispenser of information in 45-or-50-minute lectures and the student as a passive receiver, container, and repeater of the transmitted information. In contrast, learner-centered education, as the term suggests, places learners in the center of education, allowing learners to play a more active and involved role in their language study. This approach focuses on individual learners' motivations, needs, interests, and learning styles. Based on these factors, the teacher prepares lesson plans and offers different learners opportunities to work in the ways they find most comfortable and useful. The teacher is also involved in training students in their learning strategies to be autonomous and independent learners. This approach is a great challenge for both the teacher and learners. For instance, the teacher is expected to find out learners' affective factors and learning styles, and then offers different learners opportunities to work in the ways they find most comfortable and useful. According to learners' responses and performance, the teacher will substitute, supplement and adapt learning materials, classroom activities and interactions, and work with learners on an individual basis whenever possible. Meanwhile, learners must be highly independent and self-controlled.

**Major Characteristics**

1) Individual learners' motivations, needs, interests, and learning styles are respected.

2) Learners are autonomous.

3) Learners are trained to control or manage their own learning.

## 3.12  Summary

No matter what approach is, since students differ greatly, both in age and in mentality, an effective teacher should constantly revise, vary, and modify the approaches listed above on the basis of the performance of the learners and their reactions to instructional practice. A group of teachers holding similar beliefs about the approaches may implement these principles in different ways (Richards & Rodgers, 1986; Freeman, 2000). Our advice is that as a teacher, you should not be afraid to experiment with and/or adapt your style of teaching. In the end, you may discover that the best approach is eclectic in nature and includes bits of this and bits of that.

## 3.13 Questions for Discussion

1) What teaching approach appeals to you the most? State your reasons.

2) Compare the grammar-translation method and the cognitive approach that are introduced in this part and find out how they are different and similar in assumptions about language and language learning.

3) What are the advantages and disadvantages of the communicative approach?

4) How does the communicative approach differ from the direct method?

5) What level of learners do you think TPR can be best applied to?

Support your view with reasons.

6) Reflect on the way you learn English and the way you observe others learn English, and support your findings with the characteristics of the diverse learning and teaching approaches and methods.

# Chapter 4
## The Models of the Process of FLT

*Excellent teaching is made up of a repertoire of models that are very good for particular purposes but need to be assembled to generate a top-drawer learning environment for our students.*

*(Joyce, Weil & Calhoun, 2014: xvii)*

*Helping new teachers learn to help students learn is more than worthwhile. It's transporting. The satisfaction when the veil lifts and someone realized that the only barrier to growth are imaginary and self-imposed is almost unbearable. It's like watching the birth of a species.*

*(Joyce, Weil & Calhoun, 2014:3)*

Before we come to the content of language teaching, there is a need for us to get some understanding of what the process of language teaching may generally be.

Traditionally, teaching and learning were thought of as an "instructional paradigm" with the teacher as a releaser of information in 45-or-50-minute lectures and the student as a passive receiver, container, and repeater of the transmitted information. Teaching and learning were viewed as a linear process of information transfer and reception.

In fact, the process of language teaching and learning is complex and varied. Just as the diverse teaching and learning approaches of a foreign language, different paradigms of language teaching process have been formulated from different angles of these teaching approaches. It is true that a paradigm is just a paradigm, learning how to teach eventually depends on teaching itself, as what can be seen in the words of Aristotle (1985: 1103a-1103b), "For we learn a craft by producing the same product that we must produce when we have learned it, becoming builders, e.g., by building and harpists by playing the harp; so also, then, we become just by doing just actions, temperate by doing temperate actions, brave by doing brave actions." We point out here that it is impossible to list all models of teaching processes as it is impossible to cover all teaching and learning approaches in a book. Nevertheless, a closer observation can still track down the componential parts of this complex and varied process of language teaching. Hence, in this part, a brief discussion of the paradigms of the process of language teaching will be provided to facilitate effective studies and better understandings of the basic teaching acts in instructional practices in Chapter 5 and Chapter 6.

## 4.1  The PPP Model

Traditionally, language learning has been regarded as a process of mastering a succession of structures, each of which was built on the one before, such as from sounds to words, from words to sentences, and from sentences to texts. Under this notion, the most prevailing model of language teaching has always been referred to PPP model based on the assumption that a language is best presented to learners as a series of structures. The paradigm, therefore, falls into the "presentation-practice-production" paradigm, namely the PPP model.

At the presentation stage, new grammatical structures are presented in meaningful situations or contexts which best illustrate their typical uses. The teacher, as a dispenser of information, often dominates the class, doing most of the talking. At the practice stage, learners are given a variety of practice tasks in which the new language items are identified, repeated and reinforced by the learners. Teacher-guided activities, such as group work and pair work, are manipulated to motivate learners' learning. At the final production stage, learners are given practice tasks less controlled by the teacher to express their own ideas and to link what is newly learned with what has learned before.

The PPP model seems to suggest that students ready for lessons are motivated to listen to and engage with the teacher's presentation. The teacher plays a dominating role as a controller in the class. Students who are supposed to be motivated in learning should have to master "the target language in ready-to-assimilate pieces" (Foster, 1999). The communicative context is designed according to the language points to be presented. This model certainly has its use, but when it comes to closer scrutiny, it is found less effective in effecting real communication though it seems to function well at the sentence teaching level. Some radical opponents of the PPP paradigm claim that this model "reflects neither the nature of language nor the nature o learning" (Lewis, 1993) and criticizes that it represents the survival of an old behaviouristic model of teaching process combined with the relatively recent communicative view of the nature of language and communication.

## 4.2 Harmer's ESA Model

Harmer (1998) proposed a different three-stage model: Engage, Study, Activate (ESA).

During the engage phase, the teacher tries to arouse the students' interest and engage their emotions. This might be realized through a game, the use of a picture, an audio recording or a video sequence, a dramatic story, an amusing anecdote, etc.

During the study phase, activities are carried out to focus on language or information and how it is constructed. The focus of the study could vary from the pronunciation of one particular sound to the techniques an author uses to create excitement in a longer reading text. It could range from an examination of a verb tense to the study of a transcript of an informal conversation. There are many different styles of study, from group examination of a text to the discovery of related topic vocabulary, to the teacher explaining a grammatical pattern. Harmer says, "Successful language learning in a classroom depends on a judicious blend of subconscious language acquisition (through listening and reading) and the kind of study activities we have looked at here"(Harmer, 1998).

In the activate stage, the exercises and activities are designed to get students to use the language as communicatively as they can. During the activate stage, students do not focus on language construction or practice particular language patterns, but use their full language knowledge in the selected situation or task.

This model seems to place more stress upon the students' cognitive and affective factors such as interest, curiosity, and attention. The students have more room to choose a language in communicative situations or tasks. However, besides the differences, there are similarities between the PPP model and the ESA model. The study phase in the ESA model is very similar to the presentation phase in the PPP model, for both of them elaborate on presenting language points to be studied. The activate phase is partially similar to the practice and production phases, with the former emphasizing the students' freedom in using their language knowledge in selected situations or tasks, while the latter stressing the use of new language in provided contexts.

## 4.3 Ur's PPT Model

According to Ur (1996), the process of teaching a foreign language can be roughly broken down into three components: Presentation, Practice, Testing (PPT). The process of learning by means of a course of instruction has also been defined as a three-stage process: verbalization, automatization (learners perform the skillful behavior, again and again, to automatize it in a correct way, roughly corresponding to "practice") and autonomy (learners improve the set of behaviors on their own through further practice activity, sort of doing their own things).

During the presentation/verbalization phase, the teacher presents and explains new material to make it clear, comprehensible, and available for learning. He lists some guidelines on effective presentation: good preparation, make sure you have the class' full attention, present the information more than once, be brief, illustrate with examples, get feedback. At the same time, learners demonstrate or elicit the skills that the teacher has presented.

During the practice/automatization phase, the rehearsal of certain language points is aimed to consolidate learning and improve performance. At this stage, language skills and knowledge are thoroughly strengthened and mastered. This is the most important of all stages of learning; hence the teacher is expected to initiate and manage activities that provide students with opportunities for effective practice. The practice is usually carried out through procedures called "exercises" or "activities". The latter term usually implies rather more learners' activity and initiative than the former, but there is a large area of overlap: many procedures could be defined by either. Exercises and activities may relate to any aspect of language: their goal may be the consolidation of the learning of a grammatical structure or the improvement of listening, speaking, reading or writing fluency, or the memorization of vocabulary.

During the testing/autonomy phase, a test may be designed to convey how well the learner knows or can do something. The purpose of the test is to check what has been mastered and what still needs to be learned or reviewed. There are quite a few reasons for testing: give the teacher information about where the students are at the moment, to help decide what to teach next, give the students information about what they know so that they also have an awareness of what they need to learn or review, assess some external purpose of current teaching; motivate students to learn or review specific material, get a noisy class to keep quiet and concentrated, provide a clear indication that the class has reached a "station" in learning, such as the end of a unit, thus contributing to a sense of structure in the course as a whole, get students to make an effort, which is likely to lead to better results and a feeling of satisfaction, give students tasks which may actually provide useful review or practice, as well as testing, provide students with a sense of achievement and progress in their learning.

## 4.4 Willis' TBL Model

Willis' Task-Based Teaching (TBL) model is built upon sound theoretical foundations and takes into consideration the need for authentic communication. The TBL model typically falls into three stages.

The first stage is the pre-task stage, during which the teacher introduces and defines the topic and the learners engage in activities that help them either to recall words and phrases that will be useful for the performance of the main task or to learn new words and phrases that are essential to the task. This second stage is what Willis calls the "task cycle". Here the learners perform the task (typically a reading or listening exercise or a problem-solving exercise) in pairs or small groups. They then prepare a report for the whole class on how they have done the task and what conclusions they have reached. Finally, they present their findings to the class in verbal or written form. The final stage is the language focus stage, during which specific language features from the task are highlighted and worked on. Feedback on the learners' performance at the reporting stage may also be appropriate at this point. These components have been carefully designed to create four optimum conditions for language acquisition, and thus provide abundant learning opportunities to suit different types of learners. A balance should be kept between fluency, which the task provides, and accuracy, which the task feedback provides.

The main advantages of TBL model are that language is used for a genuine purpose that real communication should take place, and when the learners are preparing their report for the whole class, they are forced to consider language form in general rather than concentrating on a single form (as in the PPP model).

## 4.5  Summary

Regarding the complexity of the factors that have to be considered in language teaching, it is difficult to tell which model is more appropriate in real-time action. However, it is possible to tell, though those models all have their own focus and preference, that most of them have their common stress more or less on the following: teaching and learning, teaching theory and teaching practice, language and interdisciplinary subjects, experimentation and reflection, personal experience and others' experience.

Classroom instruction seems to go through at least three spirally progressive stages. Ur (1996) has made useful comments on the three stages. To present or instruct new material effectively is an essential teaching skill; it enables the teacher to facilitate learners' entry into and understanding of new material, and thus promotes further learning. There are several functions of an effective teacher presentation of new material in formal courses. Firstly, an effective presentation of new material makes it appear in a form that is most accessible to be perceived and understood by the learners. Secondly, an effective teacher presentation of such new material can help to activate and harness learners' attention, effort, intelligence, and conscious learning strategies in order to enhance learning.

Ur has made a thorough summary of what effective language practice should be as follows. It seems to cover a wide range of principles for designing and instructing practice activities.

### (1) Validity

The activity should activate learners primarily in the skill or material it purports to practice.

### (2) Pre-learning

The learners should have a good preliminary grasp of the language they are required to practice, though they may only be able to produce or understand it slowly. If they are required to do some practice based on something they have not begun to learn, they will either not be able to do it at all, or produce unsuccessful responses. In either case, the activity will have been fairly useless in providing practice.

### (3) Volume

The more language the learners actually engage with during the activity, the more practice they will get.

### (4) Success-orientation

We consolidate learning by doing things right. Continued inaccurate or unacceptable performance results only in the "fossilization" of mistakes and general discouragement. It is therefore important to select, design and administer practice activities in such a way that learners are likely to succeed in doing the task. Repeated successful performance is likely to result in effective automatization of whatever is being performed, as well as reinforcing the learners' self-image as successful language learners, and encouraging them to take up further challenges.

### (5) Heterogeneity

A good practice activity provides opportunities for useful practice to all, or most, of the different levels within a class. If you give an activity whose items invite response at only one level of knowledge, then a large proportion of your class will not benefit.

### (6) Teacher assistance

The primary function of the teacher, having proposed the activity and given clear instructions, is to help the learners do it successfully. If you give activity and then sit back while the learners "flounder", you are not helping. However, if you assist them, you thereby increase their chances of success and the effectiveness of the practice activity as a whole. Such assistance may take the form of allowing plenty of time to think, of making the answers easier through giving hints and guiding questions, of confirming the beginning of responses in order to encourage continuations, or in group work, of moving around the classroom making yourself available to answer questions.

### (7) Interest

Interesting activities, such an exciting topic, the need to convey meaningful communication, a game-like "fun" task, attention-catching materials, appeal to learners' feelings or a challenge to their intellect.

In short, no matter what paradigms of teaching process are, since students differ greatly, not just in age but also in mentality, classes differ greatly either in size or environment, and teaching contents and skills are received in one way or another different emphasis, an effective teacher should constantly revise, vary, and modify the paradigms of teaching processes listed above on the basis of the performance and proficiency of the learners and their reactions to instructional practice. A group of teachers holding similar beliefs about the paradigms of teaching processes may each implement these principles in different ways. Our advice is that as a teacher, you should not be afraid to experiment with and/or adapt your style of teaching. In the end, you may discover that the best paradigm in actual teaching is eclectic in nature and includes bits of this and bits of that.

## 4.6  Questions for Discussion

1) How do these models of teaching process conform to the teaching approaches discussed in Chapter 3?

2) In what ways does the PPP model differ from the PPT model?

3) How are the teacher's role and students' role different in TBL and ESA?

4) Study the seven characteristics of effective language practice that Ur introduced. Does he consider cognitive and affective factors in his summary? If so, how?

# Chapter 5
## Teaching the Language System

*Languages are viewed as nothing other than sets of social conventions by means of which human beings communicate with one another about their experience.*

*(Tomasello, 2003:18)*

*The relation of word to thought, and the creation of new concepts is a complex, delicate, and enigmatic process unfolding in our soul.*

*(Tolstoy, 1903: 143)*

## 5.1　The Language System

Traditionally, language is treated as an arbitrary system of signs and a two-fold mental entity between a sound pattern (signifier) and a concept (signified). In Saussure's view, this arbitrariness has two respects: on the one hand, the association of a particular form with a particular meaning is arbitrary, and on the other hand, the meaning associated with a linguistic form is arbitrary too. The arbitrariness of a linguistic sign is closely linked to its notion of language as a self-contained and autonomous system. The meaning of a linguistic sign is a function of the value of the sign within the sign system which constitutes a language (Taylor, 2003). That is the meaning of a word resulting from the value of the word within the system. A language structure is defined according to its properties of formal differentiation (Bloomfield 1973; Thorndike 1932). The prediction of the arbitrariness of language in a self-contained and autonomous system, and the over-emphasis on formal properties of language has influenced language teaching (first language, second language or foreign language) in many ways. Language teaching is more often than not dealt with at separate levels, each independent of the others, resulting in an over-stress upon the formal properties of language and their disassociation from the creation of useful meaning. It follows that sound practice drills, vocabulary study, and grammar rules are isolated from one another, and substitution and transformation drills are often provided to form correct habits in language. Teachers and students are discouraged from seeking motivations and regularities in the language that they learn. What they learn is just isolated linguistic signs independent of their experiences. This makes language learning abstract, hard, and grueling.

Contrary to the traditional views, language is systematically rooted in human perceptual experience and cognition. According to Langacker (1991), language is considered symbolic in nature. The relationship among sound, word, and grammar is outlined in Langacker's (1991) cognitive grammar or construction grammar. The phonological unit, semantic unit, and symbolic unit, are the three units of cognitive grammar. The symbolic unit is the conventionalized and direct association of a phonological unit with a semantic unit or a semantic unit paired with a phonological unit. Unit in cognitive grammar refers to a structure, including morpheme, word, aspect, phrase, syntactic construction, discourse, etc. These are all symbolic units. One symbolic unit is a proper subpart of another and exists independently. Langacker's assumption of the three units in cognitive grammar makes it possible to conduct a unified explanation for language and blurs the clear line of demarcation among phonology, morpheme, morphology, and syntax.

Taylor (2003) said, "Knowledge of a language is based on the knowledge of actual usage and of generalizations made over usage events. Language acquisition is, therefore, a bottom-up process, driven by linguistic experience…knowledge of a language is dynamic, and evolves in accordance with a person's linguistic experiences". Many cognitive linguists propose a usage-based model for language acquisition (Croft & Cruse, 2004). According to Robinson and Ellis (2008), "Learning language involves determining structure from usage and this, like learning other aspects of the world, involves the full scope of cognition: the remembering of utterances and episodes, the categorization of experience, the determination of patterns among and between stimuli, the generalization of conceptual schema and prototypes from exemplars, and the use of cognitive models, of metaphors, analogies, and images in thinking."

Without a doubt, this novel insight will shed an illuminating light on language teaching. The teaching of language at different levels, such as phonology, morphology, syntax, and discourse, cannot achieve its best possibility if the relationship among them is neglected. Unfortunately, the common practice in foreign language teaching is that an over-stress has long been placed upon the formal properties of language and their disassociation from the creation of useful meaning. "Drilled through substitutions or transformations, the learner was forever producing versions of a structure that represented meanings that they might never use" (Holme, 2009: 1). Such inadequacy and inefficiency of EFL teaching in China has also been a case in point. It is not difficult to find a person who has learned English for over ten years but still cannot communicate freely in English.

In instructional practices, besides the factors above in the introduction part of this book, the teacher has to take a lot more factors into consideration. For instance, he or she should be clear about the teaching content and its sequence to be carried out in instructional practice. Also, he or she should know how to borrow a pair of terms from cognitive linguistics, and to deal with the base and profile relations among the teaching contents, that is, how to guide the students to the focus (base) on learning content in appropriate profile neither beyond nor below the students' capacity. Still, a good teacher should know how to motivate his or her students with a variety of activities even though the learning content may be boring and tiring.

## 5.2  Teaching Pronunciation

> *Learners also need to develop a concern for pronunciation. They must recognize that poor, unintelligible speech will make their attempts at conversing frustrating and unpleasant both for themselves and for their listeners.*
>
> *(J. Kenworthy, 1989: 14)*

### 5.2.1  The Necessity of Teaching Pronunciation

In the teaching of English as a foreign language, there is often a low level of emphasis placed on this very important language skill —

pronunciation. Most teachers find it competent to teach reading, writing, listening and general oral skills. But when it comes to pronunciation, they often feel so frustrated that they can only offer students some rather rudimentary advice due to the lack of some basic knowledge of articulatory phonetics. For instance, when there is a need to suggest how to pronounce the dental English fricative /th/ in *those*, a teacher, without basic knowledge of how this sound is articulated in terms of manner and place, will probably advise like this, "Look, it sounds like this. Look at me and imitate." A mistaken imitation of a sound may be converted into a familiar sound in the learner's own language, which results in failure in understanding or misunderstanding in real communication. Take the /th/ sound again for example. Some EFL learners pronounce it like /s/. Correction of this sound cannot only be subject to imitation for there are slow imitators. However, if the teacher knows some phonetic rules such as how this sound is articulated in terms of manner and place, it would make things easier for both the learners and teachers. And more importantly, phonetic rules regarding how sounds are articulated can reduce the learners' time in frustrating imitation and put the learners at a jump-off point to cope with pronunciation in their independent studies.

### 5.2.2 The Concept of Pronunciation

It is not easy for most Chinese learners to acquire a total set of native-like pronunciation as what Professor Higgins wants Miss Doolittle to do in *My Fair Lady*, but it is always possible for them to achieve intelligible, smooth, natural and communicative pronunciation. What the teacher can do is to focus on phonemic contrasts and allophonic variations to ensure that the students achieve the goals of consistency, intelligibility and communicative efficiency in communication. Therefore, general knowledge of speech sounds is necessarily called forth.

The concept of pronunciation may include the sounds of the language, stress and rhythm, intonation (Ur, 1996).

## (1) Speech sounds

The speech sounds in English can be divided into two broad categories: vowels and consonants. The primary difference between a vowel and a consonant is that in the pronunciation of the former the air that comes from the lungs meets with no obstruction of any kind in the three organs of speech or cavities: the throat, the nose or the mouth, while in that of the latter it is obstructed in one way or another.

Consonants can be classified in terms of the manner of articulation and in terms of place of articulation. The following table (Table 5-1) is a brief description of the consonants.

Table 5-1  English Consonants

| Manners of Articulation | Places of Articulation | | | | | | | |
|---|---|---|---|---|---|---|---|---|
| | Labial | Labio-Dental | Dental | Alveolar | Post-Alveolar | Palatal | Velar | Glottal |
| Stops | p b | | | t d | | | k g | |
| Fricatives | | f v | θ ð | s z | ʃ ʒ | | | h |
| Affricatives | | | | ts dz | tʃ dʒ | | | |
| Nasals | m | | | n | | | ŋ | |
| Liquids | | | | l  r | | | | |
| Glides | w | | | | | j | | |

The column describes the place where the obstruction is created in producing different consonants, while the row describes the manner in which obstruction is created.

Vowels are classified in different ways. As we have mentioned, in the pronunciation of vowels, the air that comes from the lungs meets with no obstruction of any kind in the three cavities. Vowel sounds are differentiated by a number of factors: the position of the tongue, the openness of the mouth, the shape of the lips, and the length of the vowels. The following chart is a description of the four factors that differentiate the vowel sounds in English. The chart is retrieved from www. teaching-training.com. As shown in Figure 5-1, in terms of the position of the tongue, English vowels can be divided into front, central, back. In terms of the openness of the mouth, there are close, half-closed, half-open and open vowels. As for the shape of the lips, there are rounded and unrounded vowels. As for the length of the vowel, long and short vowels are included.

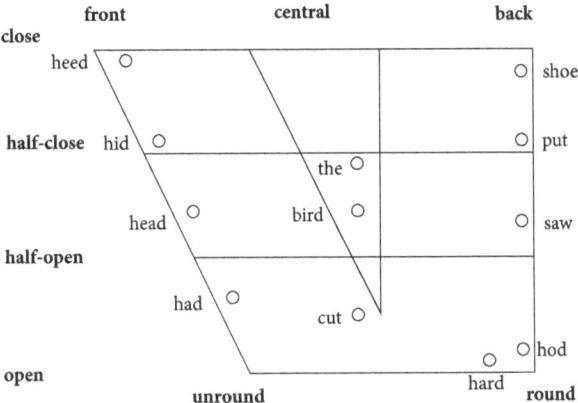

**Figure 5-1  English Vowels**

The teacher can always refer to this knowledge of sound articulation and explain to the students how to correctly and scientifically imitate a sound and quickly identify different sounds.

### (2) Stress

Stress refers to the amount of force with which a syllable is spoken. Depending on the context in which stress is considered, there are two kinds of stress: word stress and sentence stress.

Word Stress refers to a big force that is put in a syllable inside a word. English is a language in which stress is not fixed on any particular syllable of a word. Its position varies from word to word. But the location of stress in English words distinguishes meaning. For instance, usually, the noun has the stress on the first syllable and the corresponding verb has the stress on the second syllable, such as those words: *export and produce*. However, to cover the stress patterns in a book is impossible. Yet, the teacher needs to know the basic stress patterns. For instance, the following table (Table 5-2) may help in teaching pronunciation of words with more than one syllable.

Table 5-2  Part of Speech, Syllable, and Stress

| Part of Speech | Numbers of Syllable | Stress | Examples |
| --- | --- | --- | --- |
| Noun | 2-syllable | usually stress the first syllable | answer, chaos |
| | compound nouns | stress the first part | takeover, mailman |
| Verb | 2-syllable | stress the root | attend, fasten |
| | phrasal verbs | stress the preposition | take over, get up |
| Adjective | 2-syllable | stress the root | cautious, alive |
| Adverb | 2-syllable | stress the root | slowly, shortly |
| Preposition | 2-syllable | stress the root | unless, below |
| Acronym | | stress the last letter | IBM, BBC |

Sentence stress refers to the relative force that is given to the words in a sentence. In English, nouns, main verbs, adjectives, adverbs, and demonstrative pronouns are often stressed. Words like articles, person pronouns, auxiliary verbs, prepositions, and conjunctions are usually not stressed. Even positive and negative stresses are different: positive stress usually falls on the main verb. Negative stress normally falls on the main verb. But strong negative stress usually falls on the auxiliary verb.

### (3) Intonation

When pitch, stress and sound length are tied to the sentence rather than the word in isolation, they are collectively known as intonation which often makes a difference in meaning or implication. English has four basic types of intonation: falling, rising, fall-rise, rise-fall. The rise and fall of pitch throughout are called its intonation contour. When spoken in different types, the same sequence of words may have different meanings. English has a number of intonation patterns which add conventionalized meanings to the utterance: question, statement, surprise, disbelief, sarcasm, teasing, etc. Generally, the falling indicates that what is said is a straight-forward, matter-of-fact statement; the rising often makes a question of what is said, and the fall-rise often indicates that there is an implied message in what is said.

### 5.2.3 Techniques for Teaching Pronunciation

It is advisable to teach pronunciation with some drills on individual sounds. However, it is important to remember that pronunciation exercises should be put in some interesting, active, and meaningful context so that the students involved would not get bored and demotivated.

**(1) Using "odd man out"**

The teacher reads or asks the students to listen to a group of words at one time. And the students are asked to identify different words or sounds. The words are not necessarily written out. Look at the following examples:

bad   pad   bad   bad

date   Kate   Kate   Kate

## (2) Using songs

The songs to be chosen for sound practice will have to have clear pronunciation and certain sentence patterns; otherwise, the students may be discouraged if they cannot understand what the singers sing. Also, the songs you choose can be closely related to the theme you are teaching so that a deep impression may be left on the students with sufficient practice both in the song and the text. For instance, the enjoyable song: *Mary Had a Little Lamb* (The script was retrieved from *Children's Favorite Songs*).

*Mary Had a Little Lamb*

*Mary had a little lamb, little lamb, little lamb.*
*Mary had a little lamb; its fleece was white as snow.*
*And everywhere that Mary went, Mary went, Mary went.*
*Everywhere that Mary went, the lamb was sure to go.*
*It followed her to school one day, school one day, school one day.*
*It followed her to school one day, that was against the rule.*
*It made the children laugh and play, laugh and play, laugh and play.*
*Why does the lamb love Mary so, Mary so, Mary so?*
*Why does the lamb love Mary so? The eager children cry.*
*Why Mary loves the lamb, you know lamb, you know, lamb, you know.*
*Mary loves the lamb, you know, the teacher did reply.*

The teacher can first let the students listen to the song without looking at the script of the song. After one or several rounds, the teacher can give the students a handout of the lyrics with blanks in it. The students are supposed to fill in the blanks with the words or phrases that they hear. The teacher can also give the students a handout of some keywords of the lyric and ask the students to repeat these keywords while listening. If the students have difficulty in certain sounds, the teacher can explain to them how to make the sounds.

### (3) Using poems or stories or comic strips

Again, the poems or stories or comic strips to be chosen for sound practice should be simple, interesting, and motivating. It is helpful if the keywords in the selected material can be closely related to those of the text you are teaching so that a deep impression of these words may be left on the students with sufficient practice both in the poems, stories or comic strips and the text. For instance, the following is a good comic strip that can be used to teach certain sounds such as ar, oo, ou. After reading, the students can be asked to match the words that have the same sounds. It can also be used to practice stress and intonation. The following story is good for students to master stress and intonation.

*In a Dark Dark Wood*

*In a dark dark wood, there was a dark dark path.*
*And up to that dark dark path, there was a dark dark house.*
*And in that dark dark house, there was a dark dark stair.*

*And up to that dark dark stair, there was a dark dark room.*

*And in that dark dark room, there was a dark dark cupboard.*

*And in that dark dark cupboard, there was a dark dark box.*

*And in that dark dark box, there was a Ghost!*

**(4) Using riddles, proverbs, jokes, brain teasers, tongue twisters**

Sometimes it has more fun to use some riddles, proverbs, jokes, brain teasers, or tongue twisters to practice pronunciation than simply focus on individual sounds. They are usually interesting and motivating for students to overcome nervousness, shyness, and of course, boredom. The teacher can read them three or five minutes before the class ends, which will not only help the students improve pronunciation but also create a relaxing atmosphere for the students. Look at the following examples:

① *Peter Piper picked a peck of pickled peppers.*

② *A peck of pickled peppers Peter Piper picked.*

*If Peter Piper picked a peck of pickled peppers,*

*Where's the peck of pickled peppers Peter Piper picked?*

③ *A quick-witted cricket critic.*

④ *I saw Susie sitting in a shoe shine shop.*

*Where she sits she shines, and where she shines she sits.*

## 5.2.4 Summary

There are many more ideas that can be integrated into teaching pronunciation than what we can list here in a limited space. Below is a summary of teaching pronunciation.

1) Imitation of a teacher or recorded model of sounds, words, and sentences.

2) Recording of learner speech, contrasted with the native model.

3) Systematic explanation and instruction (including details of the structure and movement of parts of the mouth).

4) Imitation drills: repetition of sounds, words, and sentences.

5) Choral repetition of drills.

6) Varied repetition of drills (varied speed, volume, mood).

7) Learning and performing dialogues (as with drills, using choral work, and varied speed, volume, mood).

8) Self-correction through listening to the recording of his or her speech.

## 5.3 Teaching Vocabulary

*The relationship between thought and word is not a thing but a process, a continual movement back and forth from thought to word and from word to thought; ... thought is not merely expressed in words; it comes into existence through them.*

*(Vygotsky, 1986: 218)*

### 5.3.1  What Needs to Be Taught?

Vocabulary instruction is considered much simpler than any other instructions in language teaching as it is taken for granted that there is always a dictionary for us to consult. It is true that dictionary meaning is important for vocabulary acquisition, but dictionary meaning does not cover all the meanings that a word may have in different situations or contexts. Therefore, in order to help the students with their lexical competence, the teacher should cultivate their awareness of identifying different meanings of the same word in their English learning. In fact, vocabulary instruction is not a piece of cake at all.

In a sense, vocabulary instruction includes instruction on pronunciation and spelling. But vocabulary teaching is not just a consideration of pronunciation and spelling; the following are suggested in vocabulary instruction: meaning, grammar, formation, usage, collocation, sense relation, etc.

**(1) Word meaning**

According to Leech (1974), a word may have seven meanings:

conceptual meaning (or the sense), connotative meaning (which refers to what is communicated by the language), stylistic meaning, affective meaning (or the feeling and attitude of the speaker), reflective meaning, collocative meaning, and thematic meaning (or the organization of the message in terms of orders, forms and emphasis). All the above meanings, except conceptual meaning, are classified as associative meanings, which are the mental connection based on the contiguities of experience.

In this book, we pack the meaning of a word into three types: denotative or conceptual meaning, connotative meaning and encyclopedic meaning. Denotative meaning relates the word to the physical world or non-physical world, often referring to the meaning given in a dictionary. For example, *a dog* denotes a kind of animal. Connotative meaning is supplementary meaning extending beyond denotative meaning. It may stand for people's emotions or attitudes about what the word relates to. It may also refer to the style in which the word is used, implying the social circumstance that the word relates to. Again take the word *dog* for instance. It has positive connotations of friendship, loyalty, cuteness, for most British people but negative connotations of snobbishness, dirt, inferiority for most Chinese people. However, with the passage of time, a word's connotative meaning may change. Nowadays, the word *dog* may also connote meanings of loyalty, friendship, loveliness for some Chinese pet lovers. Encyclopedic meaning can only be achieved by activating information on certain branches of knowledge in geography, history, society, economy, politics, etc.

### (2) Word Grammar

Not every word follows general grammatical rules. In certain grammatical contexts, a word may have an unpredictable change of form, or it may have some idiosyncratic way of connecting with other words in sentences. It is therefore important to provide this information in vocabulary instruction.

1) Highlight regular and irregular forms, e.g., *think-thought, information-information (plural form), study-studies, dictionary-dictionaries*.

2) Present words with the words that often follow them, e.g., *want to, enjoy doing, responsible for, remind someone of, in front of*.

3) Introduce knowledge of word formation, e.g., *compounding, blending, derivation, backformation, conversion*.

### (3) Word Collocation

Appropriate collocation makes a particular combination of words in a given context. Therefore, it is worth attention when teaching new words that have some required collocations, e.g., *decision/take or make, conclusion/make, throw a ball/toss a coin*.

### (4) Word Sense Relation

It is useful to help the students build word nets if sense relations are introduced in vocabulary instruction.

1) Introduce synonyms, e.g., *torch/flashlight, father/dad, smile/laugh,*

*surprise/amaze.*

2) Introduce antonyms, e.g., *old/young, alive/dead, buy/sell, below/above.*

## 5.3.2 Principles of Vocabulary Instruction

### (1) Memory

Miller's experiment shows that short-term memory is of limited capacity, usually 5-9 items ("7 plus-or-minus 2"). It follows that retention in short-term memory is not effective if the number of chunks of information exceeds seven. Therefore, it is suggested that in a given time the teacher should pay attention to the memory capacity of the students. Information stored in short-term memory can become entrenched information in long-term memory by sufficient exposure and consolidation.

### (2) Basic level words

Words at the basic level are most frequently used and easy to be acquired. Therefore, priority should be given to words at this level so that the students can use them in a wide variety of contexts or situations.

### (3) Frequency

As we have mentioned at the beginning of this chapter, knowledge of a language is based on knowledge of actual usage, progressing with a person's sufficient linguistic exposure. Thus the frequency of word forms in language use is regarded as the primary factor determining the independent storage or memory of word forms. The frequent occurrence of a word form in use helps to entrench it as a conventional grammatical unit.

**(4) Regularity and productivity**

Knowledge of a language is dynamic. Vocabulary learning is not just mechanical memorization. It involves one's noticing and thinking to find out regularities that govern word forms. The opportune timing of introducing rules of word formations facilitates students' ability to regularize their vocabulary learning and to predict the meaning of new words on their own.

**(5) Network organization of word forms**

As we have introduced at the beginning of this chapter, one symbolic unit or construction is a proper subpart of another and exists independently. In this way, symbolic units will be organized in a network of taxonomy. Therefore, the teacher can guide and encourage students to group words in one way or another into word networks as schematic knowledge retained in one's long-term memory. Like the folders stored in a computer, information stored in the network will be easily activated and retrieved when needed.

### 5.3.3 Techniques for Vocabulary Instruction

**(1) Presenting new words**

There are a variety of ways for a teacher to present new words. Some are more popular than others. Some are particularly more appropriate for the presentation of certain types of words, while others are not. Different teachers may prefer some kinds of techniques rather than other ones. Here are some examples of presenting new words.

1) Direct instruction or pre-instruction. Teach specific vocabulary in reading lessons. Before reading, the teacher presents the new item with its definition, synonyms, and description. This technique is the most obvious and conventional.

2) Multiple exposures. Use visual stimuli such as pictures, drawings, word games, puzzles, cards, etc. in vocabulary instruction. It helps students to bring a word form and sound to its image of the object.

3) Using real objects. Use a real object to show the meaning of a word if it is possible.

4) Using gestures or actions to show meanings.

5) Using word formation rules and common affixes.

6) Word prediction. Ask the students to predict or guess the meaning of a word in a certain context before explaining it to them.

7) Translation.

**(2) Consolidating new words**

As we have discussed, words in short-term memory can become entrenched in long-term memory by sufficient exposure and consolidation. Therefore, consolidation work seems to be very important in this process. The following are some suggestions for consolidating new words.

1) Dictation. The teacher dictates the new words just learned. This seems to be the most convenient and conventional way of consolidating newly learned words.

2) Task restructuring. A group of letters is given for the students to restructure the word that they have just learned. Certain contexts can be provided for this type of exercise.

Example:

*John likes _____ movies. (tnaoci)*

The letters "tnaoci" should be regrouped into the word "action".

3) Blank filling. Pick out sentences from reading materials, take away the words just learned, and ask the students to fill in the blanks.

4) Matching.

Example 1:

Match column A with column B.

| A | B |
|---|---|
| *foe* | *effort* |
| *endeavor* | *enemy* |

*shield*                    *ancestor*

*convert*                   *again*

*anew*                      *change*

*forbear*                   *protection*


Example 2:

Choose the letter of the item which is the nearest in meaning to the word in italics:

A good action movie is *exciting*.

A. thrilling    B. tiring    C. interesting

5) Using word family. Give the students a group of words and ask them to group them into different families.

Example:

Put the following words into different word families.

*desk   pear   bus   apple   car   sofa   bike   orange   chair*

Vehicle:_____

Fruit:    _____

Furniture:_____

6) Word network. The teacher says a keyword and the students are supposed to write the words connected to it as many as possible in a limited period of time.

7) Odd man out. List a set of words on the blackboard or give the students a copy of word lists and ask the students to find the "odd man out".

Example:

*exciting   boring      interesting     disappointed*
*go         walk        think           jump*

### 5.3.4  Summary

There are many more ideas that can be integrated into teaching vocabulary than what we can list here in a limited space. Below is a summary of those ideas.

1) Brainstorming. Ask students to write down as many words as possible related to a specific topic that is going to be discussed.

2) Labeling. Put up drawings and pictures on the wall or the board and ask students to label the equivalent words to them.

3) Miming. Get a learner to mime the activity and the rest guess it in a given time.

4) Using synonyms and antonyms.

5) Regular review.

## 5.4 Teaching Grammar

*Without grammar you are back in the Stone Age, reduced to making the simplest of statements; or, by trying to make more complicated ones and not being able to do it, you write nonsense. Grammar doesn't exclude; not knowing grammar does. Without good grammar, you don't have full access to one of the great joys of happening to be born in this country—being able to read and write English.*

*(Mount, 2013:1)*

### 5.4.1 What Is Grammar?

Grammar is regarded as the rules to show how words are combined, arranged and changed to show different meanings, not only as the internal structure of a language but also as the structural means by which meaning and communication are realized. It is assumed in the structuralists and generative view that syntax or grammar is autonomous, independent of phonology and semantics. Grammar is the way words are put together to make correct sentences. It is more than that. Grammar is about how units of language are sequenced, since quite obviously language proceeds sequentially and linearly: in speech, one sound is uttered before the next, one syllable before the next, one word before the next, and so on; in writing, one word precedes the next, one phrase precedes the next, one clause precedes the next, and so on. So in the production of language, humans must take all their thoughts, requests, desires, and hopes that are relevant within a particular context of a situation and produce language that expresses those meanings and organizes those ideas sequentially.

Cognitive linguistics points out that the grammar of a language is a cognitive subsystem. Langacker (1987) defines grammar as a structured inventory of a speaker's knowledge of conventional linguistic units which are mostly symbolic units with their two halves, form and meaning. Phonological unit, semantic unit, and symbolic unit are the three units of cognitive grammar. The symbolic unit is the conventionalized and direct association of a phonological unit with a semantic unit or a semantic unit paired with a phonological unit. (symbolic unit = phonological unit + semantic unit) It follows that language is not autonomous at all. Grammar, semantics, morphology, and phonology are closely linked. Therefore the teaching of grammar cannot be done individually and independently without considering real contexts. Grammar should be approached as a voyage of discovery into the patterns of language with the help of the knowledge from all branches rather than the learning of prescriptive rules independent of meaning and context.

## 5.4.2 Principles of Teaching Grammar

### (1) Regularity and productivity

Knowledge of a language is dynamic. Grammar learning is not just mechanical memorization of structures and rules. It involves a person's noticing and thinking to find out what regularities govern rules or structures and how rules and structures are linked to our experience. For instance, the explanation of countable nouns and uncountable nouns can be done with an explanation of how we conceptualize the objects in the world. Take *water*, *person*, and *people* for instance. (Here we use the italicized letter to refer to words and capitalized letter to refer to the entity or object) WATER, when divided, is still WATER, and the nature of it does not change. The same analysis applies to the word *people and person*. When PEOPLE divided, they all still have the nature of man. But when PERSON divided, it is not a man at all. Therefore, *water* and *people* are uncountable nouns while *person* is a countable noun. Bringing our embodied experience into the realm of learning makes learning real and meaningful.

### (2) Context

It is important for learners to be exposed to plenty of contextualized examples of the structure. Contextualized structures which are usually instantiated and meaningful speed up learners' familiarity with these structures.

### (3) Sequence

It is crucial for the teacher to decide what structures or rules should be presented first and how the practice activities should be sequenced in communicative situations.

### (4) Frequency

Similarly, the entrenchment of grammatical rules is, to some degree, determined by the frequency of the rules in different situations. As we have discussed, knowledge of a language is based on knowledge of actual usage, progressing with a person's sufficient linguistic exposure. Thus the frequency of grammar rules in language use is regarded as one of the primary factors determining one's comprehension and productive use of the rules. The frequent of a rule in use helps to entrench it as a conventional grammatical unit.

### (5) Opportune explanation

The teacher's opportune explanation is essential to motivate learning. He or she must be clear about how to present and explain the structure's form and meaning opportunely in a way that is clear, simple, accurate and helpful. A too detailed explanation will sometimes stop learners from active thinking and discovering. It is important to teach them "how to fish" instead of just giving them fishes.

### (6) A voyage of discovery

In addition to teachers' explanations, the learners should be provided with opportunities to work out the principles or rules for themselves through a process of guided discovery. In a voyage of discovery, students may have to activate their schematic knowledge, prior knowledge and conceptual knowledge instead of pure passive reception of the information that the teacher instills. Thus they become active learners.

## 5.4.3  Techniques for Teaching Grammar

Grammar can be taught in a variety of classroom activities. The following techniques are suggested.

### (1) Awareness of grammar

After learning some grammatical rules, the students are provided with opportunities to expose themselves to those rules in extra reading materials so that they experience the use in real discourse.

If the teacher has finished teaching the past tense, he can give students extracts from other reading materials except those from the books or even newspaper articles, and ask them to find and underline all the examples of the past tense that they can find.

## (2) Awareness of context

Design some examples to train the students' awareness of the context with using rules.

Example 1:

Teaching Voice

I:   Liz is a wonderful sister. She is protective and kind toward her younger sister, Emily. But she does even more. Liz encourages Emily.

II:   Emily, being the youngest, is also the timidest. She would rarely try anything that was different or new. She has matured quite a bit, though, thanks to her sister. Emily was encouraged by Liz.


Example 2:

Function

Match the utterances with the possible situations in which they are uttered and then explain why.

a. Pardon me, sir, but would you mind opening the window?

b. Open the window, will ya buddy?

c. Open the window NOW.

d. Gee, it's hot in here.

Situations

a. Doing homework with your girlfriend/boyfriend.

b. Baby-sitting your naughty younger brother.

c. Meeting with the dean in his office.

d. Sitting on a bus next to a man dressed in work clothes.

### (3) Controlled drills

Provide students with certain situations or clues to organize sentences based on what they have learned.

Example:

Practice using forms of the present simple tense.

Choose someone you know very well, and write down his name. Now compose true statements about them according to the following model.

*He/She likes ice cream; or He/She doesn't like ice cream.*

Optional words.

a. enjoy: playing tennis

b. drink: wine

c. speak: English

### (4) Guided, meaningful practice

Learners make sentences of their own according to a set pattern, but what the vocabulary they use is up to them.

Example:

Practice conditional clauses.

Learners are given the cue "*If I had a million dollars*", and suggest, in speech and writing, what they would do.

## (5) (Structure-based) free sentence composition

Learners are provided with a visual or situational cue and invited to compose their responses; they are directed to use the structure.

Example 1:

Show the students a picture of a number of different things in different colors. And ask them to describe it.

Example 2:

Show the students a picture of a number of different people doing different things, and ask the students to describe it using the appropriate tense.

## (6) (Structure-based) discourse composition

Learners hold a discussion or write a passage according to a given task; they are directed to use at least some examples of the structure within the discourse.

Example:

The class is given a dilemma situation ("*you have seen a good friend cheating in an important test*") and asked to recommend a solution. They are directed to include modals (might, should, must, can, could, etc.) in their speech or writing.

## 5.5 Summary

In short, grammar should be approached as a voyage of discovery in meaningful situations. In grammar instruction, both meaning and form should be emphasized. The learning of structures and rules should not be independent of meaning and context.

## 5.6 Questions for Discussion

1) What are the differences among cognitive linguistics, structuralist linguistics, and transformational-generative grammar in their views of the language system? How do these differences influence the rationales of language teaching?

2) What is the relationship between meaning and form? How can we integrate these two in teaching the language system?

3) How can the usage-based model be applied to the acquisition of vocabulary and grammar?

4) What is the relationship among pronunciation, vocabulary, and grammar?

5) Why is teaching pronunciation important and necessary? Provide some techniques for teaching pronunciation according to your learning experiences.

6) Why are frequency and context important for teaching and learning vocabulary and grammar?

7) Langacker defines "grammar as a structured inventory of a speaker's knowledge of conventional linguistic units". Explain this according to your own understanding.

# Chapter 6
## Teaching Language Skills

*In order to arrive at appropriate methodologies, practitioners need to take time to investigate what happens in the classroom. They need to incorporate into their approach the capacity to look in-depth at the wider social forces which influence behavior between teachers and students, and to take a broad view of how these are in turn influenced by social forces from outside the classroom.*

*(Holliday, 1994)*

Widdowson (1978) has made reasonably convincing comments on the relationship between linguistic skill and communicative abilities in his *Teaching Language as Communication*. Traditionally, the focus of attention in language teaching and learning has been based on the language system or linguistic skills. There is a commonly held notion that once linguistic skills are acquired in reasonable measure, the communicative abilities will follow as a more or less automatic consequence. What evidence we have, however, suggests that this is not the case. The acquisition of linguistic skills does not seem to guarantee the consequent acquisition of communicative abilities in a language. On the contrary, the overemphasis on drills and exercises for the production and reception of sentences tends to inhibit the development of communicative abilities. He holds that the abilities include the skills. One cannot acquire the former without acquiring the latter. In this chapter, we discuss how the skills can be taught for communicative competence.

## 6.1  Reading

*Skilled reading clearly requires skill in both decoding and comprehension... A child who cannot decode cannot read; a child who cannot comprehend cannot read either. Literacy—reading ability—can be found only in the presence of both decoding and comprehension. Both skills are necessary; neither is sufficient.*

*(Gough, Hoover and Peterson, 1996)*

## 6.1.1　The Nature of Reading and Insights into the Reading Process

Among the generally acknowledged four language skills, reading is probably more frequently targeted in foreign language teaching research. Our conceptual knowledge about the reading process has reflected our knowledge of the nature of reading and its changes have altered some of our approaches to the teaching of reading.

It has long been asserted that, in the classroom teaching practice, reading instruction should engage in dealing with items of grammar and new vocabulary, thus ignoring the development of the students' reading abilities. It is also asserted that reading ability will develop automatically through the practice of grammar, vocabulary, and structure. In this view, classroom practice focuses too much attention on decoding the meaning of words, phrases or sentence structures rather than interpreting and understanding the message conveyed in the reading material. Materials designed for reading tasks seem to be artificial since "the intention is to draw students' attention to items of structural usage rather than to the authentic features characteristic of 'real' text, or what makes texts 'hang together'" (McDonough & Shaw, 2004). "Learn to read" is thought of as the final product in reading instruction. This conventional practice probably comes from a mistaken notion that reading is a passive activity in which the end of "learn to read" is just "to decode" instead of "read to learn". This idea was best summarized in Nuttall's reading model in 1982 (refer to Figure 6-1).

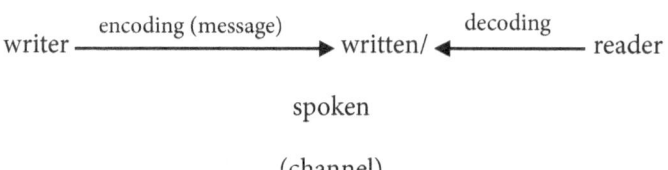

**Figure 6-1　Early Reading Model**
(Nuttall, 1982)

However, reading is more than just translating written symbols into corresponding sounds like Figure 6-1 shows. Success in a reading course requires that both the teachers and the students have a clear idea of the nature of reading. According to psycholinguistic models of reading (Goodman, 1967), meaning comes from an interaction between thought and language. Rather than decoding each word, readers select the fewest, most productive cues from the printed page that are necessary to produce guesses, and confirm them. Reading is therefore deemed as an active and creative activity. Goodman (1967) characterizes reading as a psycholinguistic process by which an efficient reader reconstructs, as best as he can on the basis of utilizing background knowledge to make predictions and check predictions against the text, a message which has been encoded by a writer as a graphic display. He summarizes that "reading always involves sampling from the physical representation in order to confirm or disconfirm predications about meaning…the meaning that the reader will eventually derive originates in his head rather than on the page".

There are two conventional insights into the reading process: a bottom-up model and a top-down model. A bottom-up reading model, also called the part-to-whole model, emphasizes a linear, part-to-whole processing of a text. At the beginning stages, little emphasis is given to the influences of the reader's world knowledge, contextual information, and other higher-order processing strategies (Dechant, 1991). Simply put, we work out the meanings of the words and structures of a sentence and build up a composite meaning for the sentence. A top-down reading model is deemed as a psycholinguistic game in which background information is firstly introduced; the reading material is comprehended by guessing the meaning of the new structures; at last new structures and words will be learned and summarized.

However, these two insights are not the whole picture of the reading process. Different from the traditional views of reading, the current reading consists of two layers. One is the visual layer, which aims to discern the signs and symbols and transmit the signal to the human brain; the other is the cognitive layer, which aims to interpret the visual information rather than get the meaning of the words. What is going on in the reader's brain is a process of reconstruction, trying to reconstruct the meaning the author attempts to express in the creative process. In fact, the second process is quite complex, rather than a passive process of receiving and interpreting information.

Brown & Yule (1983) suggest that our processing of incoming discourse can be thought of as the combination of at least two activities: the bottom-up processing and the top-down processing activities. Most researchers (Carrell & others, 1988; McCormick, T. 1988; Rumelhart, 1985; Ruddell, 1985) generally accept that both processes function simultaneously and are mutually dependent. In Rumelhart's view (1985), reading is a perceptual and cognitive process that bridges and blurs these two conventional distinctions. There comes, as a result, the interactive reading model. An interactive reading model attempts to combine the insights of bottom-up and top-down models. It recognizes the interaction of bottom-up and top-down processes simultaneously throughout the reading process, thus making itself one of the most promising approaches to the theory of reading today (McCormick, 1988).

In an interactive reading model, top-down processing parts and bottom-up processing parts describe different aspects of reading. In the bottom-up part of the reading process, we use our knowledge of the language itself to try to comprehend the meaning. For instance, a sentence is segmented into identifiable words, phrases, clauses, and meanings that are imposed upon these. At the same time, in the top-down process, we use the clues (such as context clues, prior knowledge or schematic knowledge or background knowledge) available to infer meaning from the passage. This will be seen in Figure 6-2 (the two-way arrow refers to interaction).

Hedge (2002) summarizes reading as an interactive process, a purposeful process, and a critical process. In an interactive process, schematic knowledge (including formal schemata about the organizational forms and rhetorical structures of the written text and content schemata about background knowledge, prior knowledge, world knowledge, etc.) and linguistic knowledge (knowledge about vocabulary, grammar, and idioms

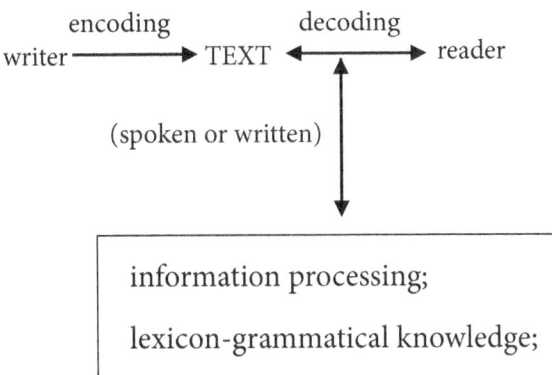

Figure 6-2　Writer-Reader Interaction

which are the foundation of the other schemata) will be activated to facilitate efficient reading. When reading is deemed as a purposeful process, "reading activities, from the beginning, should have some purpose and we should concentrate on the normal purposes of reading" such as to get information; to respond to curiosity about a topic; to follow instructions to perform a task; for pleasure, amusement, and personal enjoyment; to keep in touch with friends and colleagues; to know what is happening in the world, and to find out when and where things are (Rivers & Temperley, 1978). In a critical process, reading is viewed as a social process (Kress, 1985). It is assumed that "the ability to read critically depends on an awareness of how elements of language can be manipulated by writers". At least three principles should be observed in teaching critical reading, "teachers should not use their authority as teachers on a platform for promoting their own views; the mode of inquiry in controversial areas should have a discussion rather than instruction at its core; the discussion should protect divergence of views among participants" (Elliot, 1991).

## 6.1.2 Principles of Teaching Reading

McDonough & Shaw (2004) comment that reading as a skill is clearly one of the most important language skills and, in many instances, the most important foreign language skill. Then what principles should the teacher observe and what class procedures should be used to develop such ability?

### (1) Appropriate reading materials

At least two factors have to be taken into consideration in selecting reading materials for a reading course: interest and variety. In Williams' words, "in the absence of interesting texts, very little is possible" (Williams, 1984). A variety of topics, length of text, rhetorical organization, and reading purposes have to be taken into consideration too.

### (2) Activation of schematic knowledge

As we have discussed the nature of reading, reading should be regarded as an active process that involves the reader's active interaction with the text and the writer. While reading, the reader, instead of simply decoding the meaning of words, phrases or sentence structures, activates his or her knowledge of the language, contextual clues, prior knowledge, and world knowledge to facilitate efficient reading. It seems, therefore, very important to help students build up a solid foundation regarding these respects and cultivate their awareness of activating context clues, prior knowledge, background knowledge, and world knowledge in reading.

### (3) Purposes-orientated

The tasks designed for reading should be purposes-oriented so that the students clearly know what they are homing in on while reading. Considering differences in purposes of reading will help students build different strategies in approaching texts and different rates of reading.

### (4) Comprehension-oriented

The goals for reading should be oriented to comprehend meaning instead of simply requiring students to decode the meaning of some new words and phrases or sentence structures. Vacca & Vacca (1989) states that reading cannot take place unless the meaning is involved in the transaction between reader and writer, and comprehension is the bottom line. A reader must grab hold of and ponder over the significance of the content. Richardson, Morgan and Fleener (2008) argue that comprehension is not a passive, receptive process, but an active, constructive, reader-based process. Comprehension includes relating the text to prior knowledge, making predictions based on prior knowledge, constructing mental images, generating summaries, and monitoring when summary construction is challenging (Pressley 2000).

**(5) Integrating reading and writing**

There is a misleading notion that reading practice is for reading alone, or the end of reading practice is just "learn to read." This practice ignores Bacon's words that "Reading makes a full man, conference a ready man, writing an exact man." The teaching of reading is to facilitate students' ability to read efficiently to reach the diversified purposes that we have discussed in the nature of reading: to obtain information, to react to curiosity about a topic, to follow instructions to perform a task, to amuse themselves, to keep in touch with friends and colleagues, to know what is happening in the world, to formulate their own understandings of the underlying ideology of what they have read, etc. Therefore, an integrated instructional practice of both will ensure the students' chances to practice these two skills and to develop their reading strategies.

## 6.1.3  Techniques for Teaching Reading

Reading practice roughly falls into two types: intensive reading practice and extensive reading practice. The former is intended to train students in the strategies needed for successful reading, which involves the close study of texts, and familiarizes students with the features of written English. On the other hand, the latter is mainly concerned with operating these strategies by providing for the students' exposure to large quantities of meaningful and interesting reading materials. It can be "a useful resource to build their language competence, progress in their reading ability, to acquire cultural knowledge and develop confidence and motivation to carry on learning" and a "highly productive step towards autonomous learning" (Hedge, 2002). It is common practice to develop tasks for a reading lesson by the use of three-phase procedures: pre-stage, while-stage, and post-stage.

**(1) Pre-reading activities (schematic preparatory activities)**

1) Predicting from the title, the pictures, or keywords. Prediction is an important skill that gets the reader activated before reading.

2) Answering true or false questions before reading. True or false questions help the learners activate their schematic or encyclopedic knowledge, which will facilitate reading later.

3) Pre-questions. A general question is given before reading, asking the learners to find out a piece of information central to the understanding of the text.

4) Introducing background knowledge about the topic. Providing background knowledge broadens the learners' general knowledge, arouses their interest in learning and facilitates the forthcoming reading tasks.

5) Skimming the reading material for the main ideas. Skimming is a type of quick reading to get the gist or the main idea of the text.

6) Scanning to find specific information. Scanning is a type of reading

activity which helps locate specific information.

**(2) While-reading activities (interactive reading activities)**

1) Information transfer activities. Information in a text can be transferred to other forms such as pictures, drawings, maps, tables, tree diagrams, chronological sequence, outlines, etc. The transferred information helps the learner comprehend the meaning of the text and retain the information effectively.

2) Answering reading comprehension questions. Questions can be designed to test reading comprehension. Questions can be general or specific for the purpose of literal comprehension or appreciation, for the purpose of reorganization or critical evaluation.

3) Making inferences. It means reading between the lines and requires the learner to use background or encyclopedia knowledge to infer the implied meaning of the writer.

4) Finding the organization of ideas in a text. Work in pairs or groups to find out the organization of ideas in the text.

5) Confirming expectations or prior knowledge. While reading, the learners are required to confirm their expectations or prior knowledge that they have activated before reading and find out reasons for the difference or similarity.

6) Peer interaction. Students are encouraged to work in groups to check their understanding and construct key questions. And the teacher elicits questions from the groups and corrects them.

7) Commenting on opinions expressed in the text. This helps to build the learners' critical reading abilities so as to formulate their own ideas.

**(3) Post-reading activities**

1) Discussion questions. Students are encouraged to discuss their response to the writer's opinions to prepare for a writing activity. For instance, "do you agree with the text you read? If not, give your arguments and try to support your views with facts."

2) Reproducing the text. Students are encouraged to retell or summarize the text. Some keywords or flow of ideas can be given.

3) Roleplay. If it is in a conversational style, ask the learners to act it out.

4) Debating. Learners can be split into groups to defend their own understanding after reading.

5) Reading contrasting texts.

6) Gap-filling. Design a gap-filling exercise based on the reading material to test the learners' understanding.

7) Focusing on language points. Vocabulary or grammar can be summarized and consolidated in specific exercises.

## 6.1.4  Cases and Tasks

Case 1:
Study the following passage and work on the tasks:

- *What language points in this passage may be focused on in teaching? How will you present them before reading or after reading? Why so?*
- *What pre-reading activities will you design for the learners?*
- *Can information transfer be used to help comprehension? If so, show a few possibilities of transferring the information in the passage.*
- *What reading strategies can be employed in dealing with this passage?*
- *Can this passage involve an integrated skill? If so, in what ways can reading, speaking, listening, and writing be integrated into classroom teaching?*
- *What kind of tasks can you provide for the learners to work on after reading in class?*

### Thomas Edison

Thomas Edison was a great American inventor. He was born in 1847 and died in 1931. When he was a child, he was always trying out new ideas.

One day when he was five years old, his father saw him sitting on some eggs. He asked him why he was doing that. Tom did not answer. Instead, he asked his father:

"Hens are able to have chicks. Why can't I?"

Young Tom was in school for only three months. During those three months, he asked a lot of questions. Most of these questions were not about his lessons. His teacher did not understand his new pupil. The boy had so many strange questions. The teacher could not answer all of them. So he wanted to send Tom away from school. He told Tom's mother that Tom was not clever, and he asked her to take the boy out of school.

So Tom's mother took him out of school and taught him herself. She taught him to read and write, and she found him a very good pupil. He learned very fast. Even before he was ten, he became very interested in science.

"Mom, I want a science lab." he said one day.

"Why, Tom? What do you want a science lab for?"

"Well, you'll have to build it yourself. We haven't got enough money for that kind of thing." said his mother.

So he built a science lab himself. He grew vegetables in his garden and sold them. With the money, he bought things for his lab.

Case 2:

Study the following passage and work on the tasks:

- *How will you lead in while dealing with this passage?*
- *What kind of background knowledge or cultural background do you think worth attention? If there is any such cultural background, how will you deal with it?*
- *What reading activities can be designed to conduct teaching and learning in a TBL model?*

> *How will you integrate reading and writing skills into teaching this passage?*

**A Miserable Merry Christmas**

Christmas was coming. I wanted a pony. To make sure that my parents understood, I declared that I wanted nothing else.

"Nothing but a pony?" my father asked. "Nothing." I said.

"Not even a pair of high boots?" That was hard. I did want boots, but I stuck to the pony. "No, not even boots." "Nor candy? There ought to be something to fill your stocking with, and Santa Claus can't put a pony into a stocking."

That was true, and he couldn't lead a pony down the chimney either. But no. "All I want is a pony." I said. "If I can't have a pony, give me nothing, nothing."

On Christmas Eve, I hung up my stocking along with my sisters.

The next morning my sisters and I woke up at six. Then we raced downstairs to the fireplace. And there they were, the gifts, all sorts of wonderful things, mixed-up piles of presents. Only my stocking was empty; it hung limp; not a thing in it; and under and around it—nothing. My sisters had knelt down, each by her pile of gifts; they were crying with delight, till they looked up and saw me standing there looking so miserable. They came over to me and felt my stocking: nothing.

I don't remember whether I cried at that moment, but my sisters did. They ran with me back to my bed, and there we all cried till I became indignant. That helped some. I got up, dressed, and driving my sisters away, I went out alone into the stable, and there, all by myself, I wept. My mother came out to me and she tried to comfort me. But I wanted no comfort. She left me and went on into the house with sharp words for my father.

My sisters came to me, and I was rude. I ran away from them. I went around to the front of the house, sat down on the steps, and then crying over, I ached. I was wronged, I was hurt. And my father must have been hurt, too, a little. I saw him looking out of the window. He was watching me or something for an hour or two, drawing back the curtain so little lest I catch him, but I saw his face, and I think I can see now the anxiety upon on it, the worrying impatience.

After an hour or two, I caught sight of a man riding a pony down the street, a pony and a brand-new saddle; the most beautiful saddle I ever saw, and it was a boy's saddle. And the pony! As he drew near, I saw that the pony was really a small horse, with a black mane and tail, and one white foot and a white star on his forehead. For such a horse as that, I would have given anything.

But the man came along, reading the numbers on the houses, and, as my hopes—my impossible hopes—rose, he looked at our door and passed by, he and the pony, and the saddle. Too much, I fell upon the steps and broke into tears. Suddenly I heard a voice.

"Say, kid," it said, "do you know a boy named Lennie Steffens?"

I looked up. It was the man on the pony, back again.

"Yes," I spluttered through my tears. "That's me."

"Well," he said, "then this is your horse. I've been looking all over for you and your house. Why don't you put your number where it can be seen?"

"Get down." I said, running out to him. I wanted to ride.

He went on saying something about "ought to have got here at seven o'clock, but—"

I hardly heard, I could scarcely wait. I was so happy, so thrilled. I rode off up the street. Such a beautiful pony. And mine! After a while, I turned and trotted back to the stable. There was the family, father, mother, sisters, all working for me, all happy. They had been putting in place the tools of my new business: currycomb, brush, pitchfork—everything, and there was hay in the loft.

But that Christmas, which my father had planned so carefully, was it the best or the worst I ever knew? He often asked me that; I never could answer as a boy. I think now that it was both. It covered the whole distance from broken-hearted misery to bursting happiness—too fast. A grown-up could hardly have stood it.

(This sample text is from *College English I* by Zhai Xiangjun, Shanghai Foreign Language Education Press, 2011)

## 6.2 Listening

> *Verbal communication is a complex form of communication. Linguistic coding and decoding are involved, but the linguistic meaning of an uttered sentence falls short of encoding what the speaker means: It merely helps the audience infer what she means.*
>
> *(Sperber & Wilson, 1995:27)*

### 6.2.1 The Nature of Listening and Insights into the Listening Process

Of the commonly accepted four language skills, listening, speaking, reading, and writing, listening is perhaps the most frequently used language skill in daily life. It is estimated that we listen twice as much as we speak, four times as much as we read, and five times as much as we write! On the other hand, listening is probably the least explicit of the four skills, thus making it a big headache for most L2 or EFL language teachers and students. To promote the efficiency of the teaching of listening and enhance the students' listening comprehension competence, both teachers and students should understand the nature of listening.

In listening practice, there is a marked tendency that listeners depend too much on phonological decoding rather than on the message conveyed.

Listening ability will develop automatically through the practice of grammar, vocabulary, and pronunciation (for instance, the audio-lingual approach). It seems that "learn to listen" is the final product in listening instruction. This trend probably results from a mistaken notion that listening is a passive activity in which the end of "learn to listen" is just "listen" instead of "listen to learn".

A vast literature on listening has shown that listening comprehension is by no means a passive activity. Vandergrift (1999) states that listening is "a complex, active process in which the listener must **discriminate** sounds, **understand** vocabulary and structures, **interpret** stress and intonation, **retain** what was gathered in all of the above, and **interpret** it within the immediate as well as the larger socio-cultural context of the utterance. Coordinating all this involves a great deal of **mental activity** on the part of the listener." In his definition, listening involves the listener's active participation rather than passive decoding or reception. *(Bold letters are added by the authors of this book for emphasis.)*

Jedi Brownell (1986) suggests, in his book *Building Active Listening Skills,* six components of the listening process: **hearing** messages, **understanding** messages, **remembering** messages, **interpreting** messages, **evaluating** messages and **responding** to messages. *(Bold letters are added by the authors of this book for emphasis.)* When hearing messages, the listener learns to minimize distractions and improve concentration so that he will hear the complete message, and he also learns to prepare for various listening situations. In understanding messages, the listener discovers the importance of understanding the speaker's language and vocabulary, and the necessity for listening to the entire message. He learns to distinguish main ideas from supporting information and practices several note-taking systems. When remembering messages, the listener increases his understanding of short- and long-term memory so that he can store and retrieve information more effectively. Obstacles to effective memory are reviewed and the importance of developing creativity is emphasized. In interpreting messages, the listener better understands the speaker and his point of view by becoming sensitive to the indirect as well as the direct communication clues. He or she learns to recognize important speaker variables as they affect his interpretation of the message. When the listener evaluates messages, he or she reviews critical listening skills. The focus is on evaluating the source's credibility, speaker logic and reasoning, and identifying emotional appeals. When the listener responds to messages, he appreciates the importance of his response to what he hears and considers the effect of a variety of response styles. This model of the listening process also proves that listening is anything but a passive activity. There exists an interaction between the received messages and the listener's mind, between the message and some other factors such as the listener's linguistic knowledge, the particular situation in which it is uttered, the particular socio-cultural context, etc.

To successfully extract the intended meaning in an utterance, a listener needs to exert his or her utmost in drawing on every possible factor to interpret what he or she hears. What counts in extracting the meaning conveyed in the utterance is the listener's mental processing of the message and interaction with the context in which the utterance is made. For example, a speaker saying "It's hot in here." probably wishes to convey any one of a range of meanings: simply stating the fact that the weather is hot, or implicating to you that you'd better open the window, or expressing surprise because he/she did not expect the hotness here. What the speaker really wants to convey lies only partly in the spoken words, and the listener must try to make out the other factors that are used to carry the message to him/her.

Brown and Yule (1983) suggest that our processing of incoming discourse can be thought of as the combination of at least two activities: the bottom-up processing and the top-down processing activities. In the bottom-up part of the listening process, we work out the meanings of the words and structure of a sentence and build up a composite meaning for the sentence. In the meantime, we are predicting in the other part of the listening process, on the basis of the context plus the composite meaning of the sentences already processed, what the next sentence is most likely to mean.

As regards the listening process, top-down processing parts and bottom-up processing parts describe different aspects of listening. In the bottom-up part of the listening process, we use our knowledge of the language itself to try to comprehend the meaning. For instance, a speech is segmented into identifiable sounds and a structure is imposed upon these in terms of words, phrases, clauses, sentences, and intonation patterns. At the same time, in the top-down process, we use whatever clues (such as context clues, prior knowledge or schematic knowledge or background knowledge) available to infer meaning from the developing speech.

Based on this theory, listening instruction is assumed to fall into two models: bottom-up model or top-down model. The bottom-up model is considered as a linear process that goes, simply put, from form to meaning: firstly introduce new vocabulary and new structures, then go over the listening material, at last ask some questions about the material, check answers. The top-down model is deemed as a psycholinguistic game in which background information is firstly introduced; the listening material is comprehended by guessing the meaning of the new structures; at last new structures and words will be learned and summarized.

But it would be mistaken to maintain that they somehow are in opposition to each other. Like Brown & Yule (1983), most researchers generally accept that both models are simultaneously and mutually dependent. Therefore, the current model of listening is an interactive one in which linguistic information, contextual clues, and prior knowledge interact with each other, and enable comprehension to facilitate real-life communication.

## 6.2.2 Principles of Teaching Listening

As it is indicated in the research that we listen twice as much as we speak, four times as much as we read, and five times as much as we write, listening comprehension seems to be the most important of all language skills. The purpose of listening comprehension practice in the classroom is to effect successful communication in real-life listening. In terms of the nature of listening and in consideration of listening comprehension for successful real life-communication, what principles should the teacher observe, and what class procedures should be used to develop such ability?

**(1) Activation of the active process**

As we have discussed the nature of listening, listening should be regarded as an active process that involves the listener's active mental participation. While listening, the listener, instead of simply decoding the phonological units, interacts with what he or she hears with the help of knowledge of the language, contextual clues, prior knowledge, and world knowledge. It seems, therefore, very important to help students build up a solid foundation regarding these respects and cultivate their awareness of activating context clues, prior knowledge, background knowledge and world knowledge in the listening process.

**(2) Goal-orientated**

The tasks designed for listening should be goal-oriented within their capacity so that the students clearly know what they are driving at while listening. Clear instruction gives the students a sense of purposefulness; goals within the students' capacity are effective to observe how well the students have comprehended the listening material and also give them a sense of satisfaction and security.

## (3) Comprehension-oriented

The goals for listening should be oriented to comprehend meaning instead of simply requiring students to remember some trivial details. We have already pointed out in the vocabulary part that short-term memory is of limited capacity, usually 5-9 items ("7 plus-or-minus 2"). Hence it follows that retention in short-term memory is not effective if the number of chunks of information exceeds seven. Therefore, tasks designed for listening should be more meaning-oriented than mechanical memory.

## (4) Integration of listening and speaking

It is common in listening classroom practices that students are asked to listen to tapes with headphones and then answer listening comprehension questions. There is a misleading implication that listening practice is for listening alone, or the end of listening practice is just "learn to listen". This practice pays more attention to the non-participatory nature of listening such as in listening to a radio talk or a conference presentation, but ignores the reciprocal or participatory nature of listening such as in small talks, conversations or some other social interactions or transactions as Brown & Yule (1983) have categorized. The teaching of listening is to facilitate students' ability to effect real-life communication in which they maintain or establish social relationships or exchange information as speaking undertakes to do. Therefore, an integrated instructional practice will ensure the students' chances to practice these two skills and to develop their listening strategies.

### 6.2.3 Techniques for Teaching Listening

Listening practice roughly falls into two types: intensive listening practice and extensive listening practice. The former is intended to deal with specific items of language, sound or factual details within the meaning framework already established, while the latter mainly concerns the promotion of overall comprehension and the encouragement of learners not to worry if they do not grasp every word. These two practices have some basic distinctions: whether from general to specific or vice versa. However, we deem that though they do have some basic distinctions, in the instructional practice of the two, they can be part of the other or basis of the other. Though it is often asserted that intensive listening deals with classroom-based work, while extensive reading is an adjunctive listening program to give further off-class practice, activities for both are sometimes overlappingly used in classroom listening practice for different purposes. The following part introduces listening activities at three stages, which somewhat conform to the teaching models introduced in Chapter 4. Namely, classroom listening practice may be split into three stages: pre-listening stage, while-listening stage, and post-listening stage.

#### (1) Activities for pre-listening stage

At this stage, the teacher will need to decide what kind of listening purpose is appropriate to the listening material so that the students will not approach the listening practice with no points of reference. Activities are often to activate the students' pre-existent "knowledge schema", including the language, contexts, prior knowledge, encyclopedia knowledge, etc.

1) Predict. Before listening, the students can be asked to predict what the listening material may contain. Prediction helps to activate the students' pre-existent "knowledge schema", including the language, contexts, prior knowledge, encyclopedia knowledge, etc., which will lend a hand in the listening process. For instance, if there is a title for the listening material, ask the students to read the title and predict what the content may be. If there are pictures or photographs with the listening passage, ask the students to predict what the passage may contain.

2) Activate topic-related words. A list of topic-related words can also be learned and reviewed for the students to predict the possible content of the listening passage.

Example:

The following words and phrases will appear in this unit. All of them are related to earthquake and some are frequently used in reporting earthquakes. Listen carefully and study the definitions.

a. crust: the solid, outermost layer of the earth, lying above the mantle.

b. zone: an area or a region distinguished from adjacent parts by a distinctive feature or characteristic.

c. ...

3) Set the frame. A short reading passage on a similar topic will help to set frames of pre-existent knowledge before listening.

4) Tell true or false. A number of true or false statements based on the listening material are given to the students during or before they listen. They are supposed to tick true or false based on what they hear.

Example:

Listen to the passage carefully and tell whether the following statements are true or false.

( ) 1.

( ) 2.

( ) 3.

5) Listen for a gist. Ask the students to listen to the passage in a skimming type and then answer the gist questions based on the passage.

Example:

What is the theme of this passage?

What's the passage mainly about?

What can you infer from the italicized sentence?

### (2) Activities for while-listening stage

Activities for while-listening can always be arranged from specific to general and then to specific or from general to specific and then to general. Tasks can offer a scale of difficulties from easy to hard ones.

1) Listen and tick. The teacher asks the students to tick what they hear. The listening material can be a sound, a word, a phrase, a sentence or a passage.

Example:

Listen to the sounds and move the "odd man out" with a tick.

Tick the word or phrase that you hear.

Listen to the sentences carefully and tick what they do at school.

Listen carefully to the talk about their hobbies and put a tick for what they like.

2) Listen and fill. Ask the students to complete a grid, a timetable, a chart, a diagram, a map after their first listening.

Example:

Directions: Listen to the talk and complete the timetable below.

**Timetable for John**

| Time | Monday | Tuesday | Wednesday | Thursday | Friday | Saturday | Sunday |
| --- | --- | --- | --- | --- | --- | --- | --- |
| 9 am | | | | | | | |
| 10 am | | | | | | | |
| 1 pm | | | | | | | |
| 2 pm | | | | | | | |
| 3 pm | | | | | | | |

3) Listen and sequence. Ask the students to listen to a story or a talk and put the relevant pictures in a correct sequence.

4) Listen and locate.

Example:

You are going to listen to the talk about a student's daily activities. Listen carefully and locate the right information in the blanks.

| Event | Activities | | |
|---|---|---|---|
| | Breakfast | Lunch | Dinner |
| Time | | | |
| Place | | | |
| With whom | | | |

5) Listen and repeat. Ask the students to listen to the material and repeat what they hear.

6) Answer multiple-choice questions. Multiple-choice questions can be designed to test listening comprehension.

Example:

Listen to the whole phone call. While listening, choose the appropriate answers to the following questions.

1. How many speakers are there in the conversation?

a. 3      b. 4.      c. 5.      d.6

…

7) Answer closed-ended or open-ended questions. Sometimes questions can be discussed in small groups. Answers for close-ended questions can be found from the listening material, while open-ended questions may not be directly found from the text. For example,

Example:

You are going to hear the conversation again. Answer the following questions with the help of the notes.

1. Where did the conversation take place?
2. What was the relationship between the two speakers?
3. Why was the woman angry?
4. How did they solve the problem?
5. Who should be responsible for the broken vase? Why?

8) Dictation. Dictation can also help listening comprehension if the speed is proper.

### (3) Activities for post-listening stage

1) Note-taking and gap-filling. Ask the students to make notes of what they hear and fill the gaps with missing words.

2) Answer open-ended questions. Open-ended questions can deepen the learners' understanding of the implied meaning. Sometimes small group discussions can be organized to work on such questions.

3) Reconstruct or summarize the passage. Ask the students to work in pairs or groups or individually to reconstruct the listening material according to the notes made while listening.

4) Do a role-play. Based on what the learners listen to, ask them to do a role-play to consolidate both listening and speaking.

5) Write on the same theme. Based on notes and discussions, ask the learners to produce a piece of writing on the same theme.

## 6.2.4　Cases and Tasks

Case 1:

Study the following script and work on the tasks:

> *Identify the language points in this listening passage. Think about how you will deal with these language points in class.*
> *What listening activities will you design for the learners? Why so?*
> *Can you integrate listening with speaking in learning this material? How?*

**Going Shopping**

"Lily, I'm going to the supermarket this afternoon. Would you like to come?" asked Alice.

"Which supermarket are you going to, Alice?" asked Lily.

"I'm going to COSTCO. I need to buy a lot of things." said Alice. "Do you need anything from it?"

"Yes, I need a new pair of slippers, a few toothbrushes." said Lily.

"Well, I'm going to get two cups, a desk lamp, a few notebooks, two plastic bags, and some food." said Alice.

"All right, can we meet at 3 pm this afternoon at the front gate?" said Lily.

"Sound great. See you then." said Alice.

"Thanks, Mum. What do you need to buy in the shops?" asked Alice.

"I need to buy a watch for my son."

"I need to buy a present for Dad's birthday. I think I will buy him a computer book. I need to buy some food. I also need to buy a pair of shoes." said Mrs. Wang.

Case 2:

Study the following script and work on the tasks:

➢ *If you had no recorded material available, how could you convert this passage into a listening exercise? Try to make some practical suggestions.*

➢ *What listening activities will you design for the learners? Why so?*

➢ *Can you integrate speaking and writing in dealing with this listening material? How?*

### A Clear Conscience

The whole village soon learned that a large sum of money had been lost. Sam Benton, the local butcher, had lost his wallet while taking his savings to the post office. Sam was sure that the wallet must have been found by one of the villagers, but it was not returned to him. Three months passed, and then one morning, Sam found his wallet outside his front door. It had been wrapped up in newspaper and it contained half the money he had lost, together with a note which said: "A thief, yes, but only 50 percent a thief!" Two months later, some more money was sent to Sam with another note: "Only 25 percent a thief now!" In time, all Sam's money was paid back in this way. The last note said: "I am 100 percent honest now!"

(This sample text is from *New Concept English 2* edited by Alexander & He Qixin, Foreign Language Teaching and Researching Press, 1997.)

## 6.3 Speaking

*It needs to be said at the outset that the aim of pronunciation improvement is not to achieve a perfect imitation of a native accent, but simply to get the learner to pronounce accurately enough to be easily and comfortably comprehensible to other speakers. Perfect accents are difficult if not impossible for most of us to achieve in a foreign language anyway, and may not even be desirable. Many people—even if subconsciously—feel they wish to maintain a slight mother-tongue accent as an assertion of personal or ethnic identity.*

*(Ur, 1996:52)*

## 6.3.1 The Nature of Speaking and Insights into the Listening Process

Language is a system for the expression of meaning in human communication. Speech is regarded as the primary medium of communication over writing. Ur's (1996) assertion that speaking is intuitively the most important of all the four skills seems to echo this notion. Unfortunately, traditional EFL teaching has mostly ignored it, primarily because we over-emphasize the importance of teaching the language system only: knowledge of vocabulary and grammar rules, with little concern for language skills. It is mistakenly held that with a good mastery of vocabulary and grammar rules, speaking will automatically come its way.

With the recent growth of English as an international language of communication, there is a call for English learners who have fluency and comprehensibility in speaking English in various international situations. Speaking has become the center of the concern of teachers and learners.

Brown & Yule (1983) made a distinction between the two functions of language: transactional function and interactional function. The former is mainly concerned with the communication of information, while the latter with the maintenance of social relationships. In terms of oral communication, the language may function for different reasons: to establish and maintain social relationships and friendships, to express ideas and opinions, to solve a problem, and so on. These purposes will be achieved by activating appropriate expressions. However, as we have discussed in listening teaching, speaking is a process that cannot be dissociated from listening, as speaking can rarely happen in isolation unless it is a required oral presentation or speech delivery. Oral communication is "commonly performed in a face to face interaction and occurs as part of a dialogue or other form of verbal exchange. What is said, therefore, is dependent on an understanding of what else has been said in the interaction" (Widdowson, 1978: 58-59). Therefore, the two skills are often interdependent upon each other, and it is "this reciprocal exchange pattern which becomes important for learners to be exposed to and to practice at various stages of their foreign language career" (McDonough & Shaw, 2004).

Speaking has its own characteristics. First speaking is spontaneous. In most cases, oral interaction takes place in real-time without planning what to say ahead of time. Second, it is time-restricted. Since verbal communication takes place in real-time without planning what to say ahead of time, it allows very little time for the speaker to produce an unplanned utterance to observe the rules of conversation.

In the instructional practice of speaking skills, it is advisable for the teacher to look at the characteristics of the spoken language to meet with the requirements of the linguistic and pragmatic respects of communicative competence. Brown & Yule (1983) summarize the features that characterize spoken language: the syntax of spoken language is typically much less structured than that of written language with the former containing many incomplete sentences and little subordination. In spoken language, the largely paratactically organized chunks are related by *and, but, then,* and more rarely *if.* The occurrence of passive constructions and premodifying adjectives in spoken language is relatively rare and infrequent. A good deal of somewhat generalized vocabulary, frequent repletion of the same syntactic form, and a large number of prefabricated fillers are often used in spoken language.

Similar to listening instruction, speaking instruction has been tackled in two models: a bottom-up model or a top-down model. In a bottom-up model, teaching is started with the language systems, for example, from individual sounds to words, from sentences to discourse. In a top-down model, on the other hand, we start with an exposure to a quantity of language embedded in meaningful contexts and then comprehend and use smaller elements such as new words and structures. However, as we have discussed, speaking and listening are parts of a reciprocal exchange in which both reception and production play a role. Hence speaking is an interactive activity in which the speaker interacts with the listener and the speaking situation.

## 6.3.2 Principles of Teaching Speaking

Verbal communication, which includes both speaking and listening, as an important reciprocal exchange pattern, becomes essential for learners to be exposed to and to practice at various stages of their foreign language career. In terms of the nature and features of speaking, we have to observe at least the following principles according to which speaking is taught and the materials used in classroom instructions and practices.

### (1) Communication-oriented

Whatever activities are involved in speaking practice, it should be genuinely communicative. Genuine communication requires information gaps, in which students will show great interest and motivation.

### (2) Goal-oriented

The tasks designed for speaking should be goal-oriented within their capacity so that the students clearly know what they are driving at while talking. Tasks designed at the right proficiency level of the student are sufficient to observe how well the students have mastered the language and also give them a sense of satisfaction and security so that they will not be frustrated to give up or revert to the native language.

### (3) Accuracy and fluency

Students are encouraged to develop both accuracy and fluency in meaningful communication. Too much attention on either will prevent them from achieving communicative competence.

### (4) Authentic speaking materials

Materials chosen for speaking practice should not be artificial but authentic with a strong desire to communicate, an information gap to fill in, and a purpose to achieve.

## 6.3.3 Techniques for Teaching Speaking

In this part, we examine some techniques used in classrooms to promote the development of the speaking skills of the students.

**(1) Dialogues and role play**

Make use of authentic dialogues for pair work or group work. When the learners get familiar with the dialogues, ask them to do role play.

**(2) Information-gap activities**

Provide the learners with different information or background information and ask them to work in pairs or groups to solve a problem, or finish a task with the help of the information provided.

**(3) Interviewing**

Ask a pair of students to interview another student in class with a given task from the teacher.

**(4) Describing pictures or drawings**

Learners can be asked to work in pairs or groups to describe pictures or drawings provided by the teacher. Some keywords or expressions can be provided by the teacher ahead of time.

### (5) Retelling stories

Students can be asked to read a story and then retell what they have read in their own words.

### (6) Guided free Discussion and presentation

Students can be split into small groups and provided with a broad topic for discussion. And after that, some students are invited to do class presentations.

### (7) Problem-solving

For instance, the learners are given the character profiles of four different students, each of whom wishes to be elected as a student union leader. Discuss in groups or pairs whom they want to select, giving their reasons in each case.

## 6.3.4 Cases and Tasks

Case 1:

Starting and finishing conversations and showing interests

Task 1: Study the following patterns used in starting and finishing conversations and showing interests.

*Sorry to interrupt but     is this your ...?*

*Excuse me,          didn't we meet in …?*

                         *aren't you…?*

                         *I hear you're a…?*

*Really? Do they? Is she? Mmmm…*

*How are you getting on with the…?*

*What was the … like?*

*What did you think of the… ?*

*How interesting, but how…?*

*Tell me about the….*

*Will you excuse me, I'm afraid I must go and*

        *see if ….*

        *say hello to….*

        *get on with….*

*Let's talk more at lunch. I gotta finish up this presentation before 10:00.*

*Sorry, I can't talk longer. I'm actually on my way to meet my friend for coffee.*

*It's been very interesting talking to you.*

*I've enjoyed hearing about…*

*Anyway, it was good seeing you. I'll let you go back to your work.*

*I'd better go and…*

*See you again soon, I hope.*

Task 2: Make dialogue according to the situations given below.

Situation A: You are sitting in a bar. A friend arrives with two companions and introduces you. After a short time, you have to leave. What do you say?

Situation B: You are at your friend's dormitory. She wants to tell you about her weekend, but you are in a hurry. What do you say?

Case 2:

Developing dialogues

Work in a group of three and describe to your partners what animals you like and dislike, and explain why. Use the patterns provided.

*I like ... because....    I don't like...because ....*

*She likes ...because .... She doesn't like...because....*

*He likes ... because .... He doesn't like...because....*

*We all like...because....*

*We all don't like...because....*

## 6.4  Writing

*A text is explicit not because it says everything all by itself but rather because it strikes a careful balance between what needs to be said and what may be assumed. The writer's problem is not just being explicit; the writer's problem is knowing what to be explicit about.*

*(Nystrand, Doyle & Himley, 1986:81)*

## 6.4.1 The Nature of Writing and Insights into the Writing Process

Language is a system for the expression of meaning in human communication. Though writing is considered as the secondary media of communication, writing seems to be as important as speaking for "writing makes an exact man."

Widdowson (1978) argues that writing cannot only be the use of the visual medium to manifest the graphological and grammatical system of the language, or in one sense, the production of sentences as instances of usages. Writing is a complex thinking process in which writers explore thoughts and ideas and present them in visible words. Writing does not only have something to do with vocabulary and grammar, but also, more importantly, has something to do with individual thinking, which is an intellectual and emotional exhibition. Reasonable thinking leads to good writing, while muddy thinking can only result in muddy writing.

However, in a foreign language learning context, writing has been regarded as one of the most difficult areas for the teachers and learners of

English to tackle. Similar to reading, there are also two pedagogical insights of writing: a bottom-up model and a top-down model. In bottom-up model, writing, product-oriented, was traditionally deemed as a linear process in which students were asked to engage in predetermined tasks or exercises to practice knowledge of specific grammatical and lexical patterns. It was viewed as a fairly one-dimensional activity in which accuracy in vocabulary, grammar, and sentence structures was all the more important. The way the teacher responds to students' writing is to identify and correct mechanical errors such as spelling and grammar. Initiating ideas and reflecting thoughts are overlooked to a great extent. Thus both the teacher and students are discouraged from writing courses. The teacher seems to only play a role in spotting grammatical errors and reinforcing a set of grammar rules. The students become mechanical practitioners of grammar exercises in controlled contexts. Writing is not respected as an active cognitive process at all. In Tribble's words, students were purely "writing to learn" as opposed to "learning to write" (Tribble, 1996). Simply speaking, we work with the words and structures of a sentence to construct a written discourse that matters nothing if it does not reflect our thoughts or whatever.

In a bottom-up model, writing is thought of as a linear process. Contrarily, in a top-down model, writing is viewed as a generative, recursive, cognitive process, which stresses on the creativity of the individual writer and the development of good writing practices, rather than the imitation of models (Tribble, 1996).

Recently there is a call for an integration of product and process, for it is important to balance out process and product, fluency and accuracy, content and form.

The literature on the procedures of writing is varied. McDonough & Shaw (2004) have summarized the complex procedures of writing that many types of research (Payne, 1969; Hedge, 1988; Byrne, 1988; White & Arndt, 1991) had listed for teaching purposes:

1) Pre-writing. Jotting down ideas and preparing provisional plans.

2) Drafting and redrafting, involving reviewing and revising; in other words, working out what to say and then how to say it best.

3) Editing the pre-final version, including assessing clarity for the intended readers and checking accuracy.

### 6.4.2 Principles of Teaching Writing

#### (1) Communication-oriented

Whatever writing activities are involved in classroom practice, writing should be genuinely communicative. Student writers should be encouraged to develop writing proficiency for not only linguistic consolidation but also communicative goals. In such a case, writing tasks that are authentic for communication interest and motivate students.

#### (2) Integration of process and product

In EFL teaching, as our students are language learners rather than writers, accuracy seems to be an important and necessary requirement for the final product. However, even though writing partially serves as reinforcement and consolidation for the learning of the language itself, the nature of the process of writing itself should not be underestimated.

### (3) Teacher's role

The teacher's role should vary in teaching writing. He should not just be a judge, a critical evaluator of the final product, but also a "motivator" and "feedback provider".

### (4) Integration of the four language skills

Since our students are language learners, in teaching writing, it is advisable to combine reading, speaking, and listening into writing. Pre-writing reading, discussion, collaborative work, peer critics, which all help activate students' schematic knowledge in writing, obviously involve not just writing alone.

### (5) A sense of mistakes and errors in the correction

On weighing students' writing, the teacher should make a distinction between "mistakes" and "errors". Mistakes that are self-corrigible can be overlooked, while errors, which are largely the outcome of a learner's developing competence, require direct feedback and remedial treatment.

### (6) Purposes-oriented revision

Revision should be oriented for not only improving language skills but also helping students improving communicative abilities, logical organization, genre-appropriateness, etc.

### (7) Integrated assessment

The way we evaluate student writing should not be one-fold. There is a need for an integrated assessment of both formativeness (the concern for a developmental process) and summativeness (the evaluation of the end-product) for writing.

## 6.4.3 Techniques for Teaching Writing

In this part, we examine some techniques used in classroom writing instructions to promote the development of writing skills in the students.

### (1) Generating ideas

When students are asked to generate ideas about a topic, individual or solitary activity can be arranged for students to take inventory from activating their prior knowledge, ask questions to look for relationships between ideas and thoughts, qualify the area that can be chosen to defend. Varied activities can be used for this purpose: brainstorming, free-writing, clustering, listing, tree-diagramming (Payne, 1969).

**(2) Reading activities**

As we have discussed, reading and writing are closely linked to one another. Without sufficient exposure to how ideas and thoughts are manifested in that language, it is hard for anyone to produce good work in that language. Reading, as a precursor, also activates students' prior knowledge and helps to reconstruct their schematic blocks for writing purposes.

**(3) Group discussion or pair work**

Writing and the other three language skills can be integrated to improve language skills at an overall level, to exchange and qualify ideas and thoughts, to reconstruct their schematic knowledge.

**(4) Composing and drafting**

Composing and drafting are often carried out on the part of the student without readership. But it does not mean that the students spend time writing alone. The teacher can provide in a well-structured way positive intervention and support in the development of writing skills, such as how to generate ideas, how to draw an outline, how to develop reader awareness, how to distinguish and make different types of writings, and so on.

## (5) Revising and rewriting

The teacher may revise tasks alone or require peer revision, students' self-revision. Revision considers the following factors: communicative quality, logical organization, layout and organization, grammar, vocabulary, handwriting, punctuation, and spelling (those headings are suggested in Hopkins & Tribble, 1989). The above factors do not have to be handled in stages according to the students' proficiency.

### 6.4.4 Cases and Tasks

Case 1:

Descriptive writing

Task 1: Ask the students to describe what's in the picture and what they are doing. The teacher writes down the keywords and sentence patterns on the blackboard that the students are supposed to practice.

Task 2: Work in pairs to describe the picture.

Task 3: Write a short passage to describe what you see in the picture, using the words and sentence patterns provided.

Case 2:

Story writing

Task 1: Work in pairs at the beginning of a story and discuss what could happen then.

*One cold wet night, the farmer got out of bed and went outside. Then...*

Task 2: Ask the students to finish the story by himself of herself.

Task 3: Share their stories in class.

# Chapter 7

## Lesson Planning and Classroom Management

*[It] is generally the teacher who creates the working atmosphere of a class. If you [teacher] over-dominate, the students tend to invest little of themselves in the class, and you may even have discipline problems. On the other hand, if you fail to direct the students when necessary, and give firm guidance, they are likely to make an ineffective working group and suffer feelings of frustration and insecurity.*

*(Gower, Phillips & Walters, 1995:59)*

## 7.1 Lesson Planning

We have discussed different paradigms of the process of language teaching in earlier modules in Chapter 4: PPP, ESA, PPT, and TBL. In this chapter, we will first look at the necessity of lesson planning and the components of a lesson plan, discuss the principles for a good lesson plan, and at last, illustrate the packaging of such components in several sample lesson plans.

### 7.1.1 The Necessity of Lesson Planning

Teaching is an art of complexity. Successful teachers are skilled planners, observers, thinkers, and meditators. Lesson planning is a special skill that a teacher needs to help on the level of better engagement and a better learning process with their students. Creating lesson plans is a way of thinking, communicating, and meditating. It is essential for both inexperienced and experienced teachers to make decisions in advance about the teaching content, learning objectives and goals of the lesson, instructional procedures, and stages, techniques and activities for each procedure and stage, time allotment, student assessment in the class. It takes some time to hone this skill in the actual teaching environment by learning, observing, practicing, and reflecting. No one can gain it overnight. Language teachers can always benefit from lesson planning in several ways. Developing lesson plans helps the teacher to have a clear understanding of the goals and objectives of the lesson and its teaching contents. It also helps the teacher to accommodate different instructional procedures of a lesson and techniques for each stage. Moreover, a teacher can think about in advance how much time should be allotted to different stages of a lesson and make sure that everything planned is to be covered at a given time. Also, a teacher can think about what equipment and aids are needed and available for the lesson. Besides, developing a lesson plan helps a teacher to determine what kind of assessment will be used for the students and what sort of homework can be used to extend classroom activities. It is said that knowing "how to" is far more important than knowing "what is about" when it comes to lesson plans. And it is one of the essential markers along the way to becoming a professional teacher.

## 7.1.2 The Difference between Global Planning and Local Planning

Lesson planning can be done at two different levels: global planning and local planning. Wang Qiang (王蔷, 2000) used macro planning and micro planning to describe the two levels of lesson planning. Macro planning is explained under the following headings:

*Knowing about the course;*

*Knowing about the institution;*

*Knowing about the learners;*

*Knowing about the syllabus.*

In terms of global planning, we mean an overall decision made about the teaching and learning program. The teacher shall consider the following: learners (age range, sex ratio, social backgrounds, motivations, attitudes, interests, learning needs, current proficiency level, and other individual factors), the course (the sequence of language areas, units, skills, or topics in a course), the requirement and situation of the institution or the state, and the syllabus (including the development of goals and objectives, the selection of teaching and learning activities, and the evaluation of the outcomes of the program). It is very similar to curriculum development and design, or educational programs made for each course.

In terms of local planning, we mean a detailed teaching plan for each specific lesson that is generally less than 50 minutes. A local lesson plan, based on global planning, shall contain such components as objectives, language contents and skills, instructional procedures and stages, teaching aids and equipment, assignment and evaluation. It will be handled in the following part.

There is no clear cut difference between these two levels. Global planning directs local planning and is modified and accommodated according to how the lessons turn out.

## 7.1.3  Components of a Lesson Planning

There are varied models of lesson planning and principles of curriculum and instruction, among which the dominant one is the rational-linear framework proposed by Tyler (1949). It contains four sequential steps: specify objectives, select learning activities, organize learning activities, and specify methods of evaluation. However, other scholars found that the sequence was not strictly followed since the teacher focused mostly on the interests and needs of their students. Li Tingxiang (李庭芗, 1983) suggests that lesson planning generally includes three aspects: to prepare the material, to prepare the students, and to prepare teaching techniques. Wang Qiang (王蔷, 2000) in her book comments on three components: teaching aims, language contents and skills, teaching stages and procedures. Shu Baimei (舒白梅, 2005) points out six elements of a lesson plan: goals, objectives, materials and equipment, procedures, evaluation, and follow-up work/homework/extra-class work. From the above components of a lesson plan, it is not hard to notice that components have become more detailed, which are caused partly by the changes of teaching theories and teaching framework, and partly by the development of modern science and technology, such as the emergence of computer and the Internet. Therefore, a good lesson plan contains goals and objectives, language contents and skills, instructional procedures and stages, teaching aids and equipment, assignment and assessment. These components will be better illustrated in the sample lesson plans.

In this part, we will first illustrate the connotative meaning of the components of a lesson plan and then exemplify them in sample lesson plans.

### (1) Goals and objectives

A distinction exists between "goals" and "objectives". The former is taken to refer to the general and broad purpose for a course stated in the syllabus, which is usually set out in a national or institutional curriculum. The latter, on the other hand, states the specific purposes that will be achieved from the lesson.

### (2) Language contents and skills

A successful teacher always knows exactly what language to be taught and what language to be practiced in a lesson. Language contents may consist of the language system (including pronunciation, vocabulary, and grammar) or the more communicative categories (events, topics, culture, situations, notions, and functions). Communicative categories can easily be overlooked and put in a secondary place, though not in all cases. However, from our discussion about teaching the language system and the language skill, it is obvious to find that these contents do not come in independently, but in a combination. For instance, topics and situations provide a context for the teaching of the language system, while the language system is learned to carry out communicative activities. Language skills mainly refer to communicative skills involving in listening, speaking, reading, and writing as we have discussed in earlier parts.

### (3) Instructional stages and procedures

Stage refers to the global steps that a teacher will go through in the classroom, while procedure refers to the local steps in each stage. Generally, the paradigms of the teaching process define instructional stages and procedures. They are sort of guidelines for the teacher to make decisions about instructional procedures and stages for each lesson, such as what we discussed in Chapter 4. For instance, PPP, ESA, PPT, or TBL are the global steps in classroom practice. Some are in a structure-based dimension, while others are in a skill-based dimension; some are in a topic-based dimension, while others are in a task-based dimension. However, it does mean that one, exclusive of others, functions in actual teaching. There are no fixed, invariable procedures and stages for all. Based on these dimensions, a number of options for deciding procedures and stages are available, and the teacher will need to decide what is best and suitable for his or her students. That is, in consideration of individual factors, e.g., learners' differences, teaching contents and skills, students' reactions to instructional practice, their proficiency level and performance, instructional procedures and stages may be revised, varied, and modified. You may find that eclectic of nature in actual teaching which includes bits of this and bits of that.

### (4) Teaching aids and equipment

Traditional classroom instruction in China is characterized by a textbook for both the teacher and students, a teacher lecturing, students listening and taking notes, and a blackboard. Teachers may use real objects, drawings, wall pictures, flashcards, and imaginary objects (through mime and gesture) as teaching aids. As scientific advances bring modern technology into the domain of educational reality, most schools are equipped with advanced electrical audio-visual equipment such as tape recorders, overhead projectors, videotapes, the Internet, and computers. Therefore, the concern is growing about what kinds of teaching aids and equipment will be used in classroom practice, such as tape recorder, video, the Internet, computer, etc.

**(5) Assignment**

Assignment refers to the extensive practice and production of classroom activities in students' off-class hours. It consolidates teaching and learning.

**(6) Assessment**

Assessment in ELT (English Language Teaching) refers to "the general process of monitoring or keeping track of the learners' progress" (Hedge, 2002). When assessment comes to the minds of most teachers, it is probably a one-fold one—testing. In fact, assessment is a more inclusive term, "a multifaceted concept" (Hedge 2002). Testing is one typical kind of assessment which is formalized and standardized to collect information about the students' learning under certain situations. The latter is "integral to the whole process of teaching and learning" (ibid). In *Affect in Language Learning*, Arnold (1999) points out the difference between standardized testing and authentic assessment. The former emphasizes the weakness of failures, i.e., what students cannot do, while the latter highlights the strengths or progress, i.e., what learners can do.

With different purposes in different learning contexts (e.g., learning the language system, language skills, or integrated skills), assessment can be varied to gather appropriate information. Assessment can be done at various times throughout a program, and a comprehensive assessment plan will generally include formative and summative assessments. Simply put, the former, pedagogically motivated, is "learner-centered, teacher-directed, mutually beneficial, formative, context-specific, ongoing, and firmly rooted in good practice" (Angelo & Cross, 1993). It focuses on the process of learning, thus providing information about a learner's progress as the immediate basis for further classroom work. The latter, which fits into the administrative requirements of an institution, focuses on the result of learning and provides accountability.

Hedge (2002) also points out the third purpose for assessment—formal certification. For instance, for non-English majors in China, there are CET 4/6 and PETS, while for English majors, there are TEM4/8, and all kinds of proficiency tests, administrated by different educational testing services.

Classroom assessment, as one of the most common formative assessment techniques, is designed to help teachers find out what students are learning in the classroom and how well they are learning it. The purpose of this technique is to improve the quality of student learning, the improvement of instructional quality and curricular modifications. Hedge (2002) lists four procedures of classroom assessment: paper-and-pencil tests, structural classroom observation, portfolio and self-assessment.

In China's National English Curriculum 2017, experts list nine principles to conduct the assessment in China. They are, by all means theoretical achievement in assessment reform. The nine principles are as follows. First, the assessment should be given a full play. Second, students should be put in the center of the assessment system. Third, the content and standard of assessment should be conducted by following the goals of the curriculum. Fourth, the assessment should be conducted reasonably and appropriately with various means. Fifth, the formative assessment should be used to monitor and promote the process of teaching and learning. Sixth, the summative assessment should be used to test students' comprehensive language ability. Seventh, the relationship between teaching and assessment should be properly managed. Eighth, the formative assessment is suggested to be used at the elementary level to promote students' interests in learning. Ninth, the summative assessment should be properly designed for junior students' English academic examination.

## 7.1.4 Principles for Lesson Planning

In making lesson plans as making the plan for any other event, we need to follow certain principles or guidelines to make it work well in actual teaching.

Ur (1996) offers the following principles for ordering components of a lesson.

1) Put the harder tasks earlier.

2) Have quiet activities before lively ones

3) Think about transitions.

4) Pull the class together at the beginning and the end.

5) End on a positive note.

Wang Qiang (王蔷, 2000) suggests that a good lesson plan must suffice the following principles: variety, flexibility, learnability, and linkage. Shu Baimei (舒白梅, 2005) has an alternative listing of the principles: variety, sequencing, pacing, timing, and flexibility.

Besides the agreed points, they all emphasize particularly on one aspect or another. No matter whose definition it is, in creating lesson plans, we have to watch at least these principles.

### (1) Goals and objectives-oriented

Based on the knowledge of the teaching contents and skills, students' needs and proficiency level, students' response to formal instructional practices, and time constraints, the teacher should be clear about what goals to achieve for the course and objectives to fulfill in a specific lesson.

### (2) Variety

A variety of activities to introduce learning content will motivate and interest the students in a lively learning environment.

### (3) Selection and sequence

First tasks and activities designed for a lesson should be appropriately selected and logically sequenced to accommodate to the goals and objectives decided for the lesson, the students' language proficiency, students' psychology, and the real situation of the learning environment, etc.

### (4) Transitions

It is helpful to have very brief transition activities to make smoother the move from one stage to another.

### (5) Time allotment

Think in advance how much time will be allotted for different procedures, stages, or activities. It is useful for off-class self-assessment to make the lesson plan better.

### (6) Flexibility

It is always advisable to plan more than what you need with several options. When negative responses come from the students to one option, you still have another to switch to according to specific situations.

## 7.1.5 Lesson Plan Samples

Sample 1:

**First Aid (45 min.)**

**Objectives:**

a. to have the class acquire some right knowledge about first aid and know its importance;

b. to have the class get familiar with the use of modal verbs to express their opinions in different situations.

**Important points/grammar:**

a. New words and phrases;

b. Modal verbs: must and should.

**Procedure**

**Warm-up/Lead-in activities (approx. 3 min.)**

Using pictures to lead in the text.

**Stage 1: presentation(approx. 10 min.)**

Discussion: discussing with the students what they will do if the accident in the picture happens.

Sharing reading: reading the text together with the students and compare their solution to what has been written in the text.

**Stage 2: practice(approx. 12 min.)**

Reading the text the second time.

Forming short answer Q's (choral work).

Forming longer answer Q's. Ask the students to use modal verbs to express their ideas (pair work).

Checking students' work.

**Stage 3: production** Guided, meaningful production (**approx. 17 min.**)

Pair work: students work in pairs according to a given task regarding the different contexts in need of first aid; they are directed to use at least some examples of the structures within the discourse.

Written work: students work in pairs for written dialogues based on their given tasks; they are directed to use at least some examples of the structures within the discourse.

Volunteer pairs are invited to act out in front of the class.

**Reserved activities:**

Providing supplementary reading to practice *Should and Must* in the real context.

Picture description in pairs or groups.

**Homework:**

Supplementary reading related to first aid (**approx. 3 min.**)

**Teaching aids:** pictures, slides, pieces of paper with different tasks on.

**Assessment:** Omitted

Sample 2:

**How to Find True Love (90 min.)**

**Objectives:**

a. To be able to know the features of a familiar style;

b. To understand what true love is and discover the features of true love and ways to find true love.

**Difficulties:**

a. Features of the familiar style;

b. Some special expressions used in daily life;

c. Reading strategies: skimming, scanning and critical reading.

**Teaching procedures:**

**Step 1: warming-up (approx. 15 min.)**

a. initiate the students to define what true love is according to their own experiences (**activate prior knowledge**);

b. ask the students to tell what true love is according to the author (**skimming and scanning**).

**Step 2: discuss the text (approx. 25 min.)**

a. discuss the story in terms of organization, theme, language (**discovery** of features of the familiar style);

b. compare what they think about the topic and what the author thinks about it (**critical reading** to form their ideas).

**Step 3: compare the content of the story, the song "What is a wife" and the video clip "If Only"(deep study) (approx. 45 min.)**

a. listen to the song "What is a wife" and take notes (approx. 3 min.) **(integrated with listening)**;

b. watch the video clip "If Only" and take notes (approx. 5 min.) **(integrated with listening)**;

c. ask the students to think critically and compare the content of the story with those of the movie and the song. (approx. 12 min.) **(reading for critical thinking)**.

Consider:

a. How does love reveal, on a grand scale or on a trifle scale?

b. What's your definition of true love?

c. What would you do in search of true love?

d. Ask the students to work in pairs (approx. 15 min.) **(integrated with speaking)**;

e. Volunteer class presentation (approx. 10 min.) **(integration)**.

**Step 4: follow-up research and discussion (approx. 5 min.)**

a. teacher's comment;

b. supplementary reading and more independent research on the topic **(extensive reading)**;

c. finish an essay under this topic **(integrated with writing)**;

d. peer evaluation of their written work before handing in.

## 7.2  Classroom Management

Surveys and research indicate that many beginning teachers have a sense of inadequacy in managing their classrooms. Similar to lesson planning, this skill does not acquire overnight and has to be honed in actual teaching experiences. The skills associated with effective classroom management are only acquired with practice, feedback, and a willingness to learn from mistakes. Due to the heterogeneity of every instructional actualization, there seems to be no one best solution for all. But still, theoretical researches and experiences from classroom teachers with many years of experience may contribute to an understanding of what works and what does not work in classroom management.

Classroom management is the strategy that teachers need to organize complex classroom life to create a positive learning environment. Richards (1990) states that classroom management refers to how student behavior, movement, and interaction during a lesson are organized and controlled by the teacher to enable teaching to take place most effectively." McDonough & Shaw (2004) use the term "structure" to refer to classroom management. It is "concerned with how classes are managed, and thus with decisions about various classroom options as to who works with whom and in what possible groupings"(McDonough & Shaw, 2004). From their definitions, we can find that classroom management has something to do with the teacher, the students, and teaching activities. However, as modern technology has been introduced into the domain of the classroom reality, new equipment has become one of the concerns for classroom management too. Therefore, classroom management may include the management of relationships, the management of language, the management of interaction, and the management of equipment. In all the four types, the teacher and the students play important roles.

## 7.2.1  The Management of Relationships

Ur (1996) defines the lesson as "a type of organized social event that occurs in virtually all cultures." As lessons may vary in topic, time, place, atmosphere, methodology, and materials, teacher-student relationships, student-student relationships, activity-purpose relationships, and equipment-student relationships may also change. For instance, in what setting should pair work, group work be organized? In what situation should listening activity and speaking activity be integrated? In what practice should the teacher take the lead? …These are all the central concerns for teachers.

## 7.2.2  The Management of Language

By the management of language, we mean the teacher's language arts, including body language and utterance. A successful teacher knows how to initiate his or her students verbally and nonverbally, explain things in detail or concisely, express a sense of humor, motivate the students by showing expectations, and give the students a sense of fairness and justice. A proverb goes like this, "Those who teach well can speak well." It is true for language teachers. Language is a very subtle art which, when properly refined, can create a harmonious, enjoyable, comfortable, and positive learning environment, which in turn enhances teaching and learning. For instance:

**General questions**

*Can you all hear me?*

*Have you all brought your books?*

**Checking instructions**

*Who is in group A?*

*What do you have to do?*

**Progression of activities**

*Have you finished?*

*Are you ready?*

*"Please, look at the overhead projector and read the first line with me. I need to see everyone's eyes looking here."*

### 7.2.3　The Management of Interaction

Classroom interaction ensures how the activities will be effectively carried out for the efficiency of teaching and learning. However, it is not surprising to know that more often than not, most teachers, regardless of their experience, have difficulty in initiating and managing effective interaction, which facilitates successful learning.

Conventionally, classroom interaction is characterized by the "IRF" (Initiate-Respond-Feedback) model in which the teacher initiates an exchange usually in the form of a question, and a student answers, then the teacher gives feedback (assessment, correction, comment), and initiates the next question (Sinclair & Coulthard, 1975). McDonough & Shaw (2004) put it alternatively as a lockstep organization of classroom interaction: it is in a simple sequence of teacher stimulus—student response—teacher evaluation of student response.

Some educationalists believe that interactions between students and teachers are fundamental to the learning process. However, just as the different relationships in everyday classroom practice, research shows that classroom interaction is not a unilateral action and reaction, but a reciprocal process. Classroom interaction is also a multifaceted one, which involves more than just the teacher-student interaction. As Long (1975) critically commented that if a teacher asks the students to "cover the same ground at the same time, at the same pace, via the same approach, method and techniques, and using the same material," he will be "unemployed" at any time. As to the growing concern about cognitive factors, affective factors and a lot more other factors (modern technology for instance), the classroom interaction patterns, besides teacher-student interaction, may also include the interaction between students, the interaction between students and learning material, the interaction between students and learning environment such as multimedia, the Internet. In today's language classroom, teachers do not always organize students as one big group but break the class down into smaller size units. The most common student groupings are lockstep or closed-ended teacher questioning, pair work, group work, choral responses, collaboration, or individual work (Ur, 1996; McDonough & Shaw, 2004; Wright, 2005).

In the multifaceted interactions, on the one hand, students involve themselves in active, positive, flexible, and dynamic classroom activities. As a result, their learning motivation and interest will be correspondingly enhanced. Diverse interaction patterns diversify teachers' roles. They are not fronted in the classroom as a lecturer, rather a planner, a controller, an assessor, an organizer, a prompter, a participant, a resource-provider (Harmer, 1983). But we have to keep this in mind: sometimes in collaborative work such as group work or pair work, some students will probably provide lower-level language models. Or even some students "practice" their mother tongue instead of what they are supposed to do. Or the students are carried away and cause problems of class control. Or in a too big class, organizing group work or pair work will not seem to be possible. Or the institution authority has strong objections to what is practiced in the classroom. Then, the teacher has to work out the reasons for these problems.

If they cannot be solved, alternative ways should be used to accommodate the situations.

### 7.2.4   The Management of Equipment

As modern technology is introduced into the domain of the classroom reality, the equipment has become one of the concerns for classroom management, too. Nowadays, most schools are equipped with tape recorders, overhead projectors, video, the Internet and computers. For instance, how to manage the multimedia and the Internet-assisted classroom, when to use the multimedia and the Internet, how to organize activities involving students through the multimedia and the Internet become concerns of the teacher in a language classroom.

### 7.2.5   Discipline in the Classroom

So far, we have discussed classroom interaction patterns, but things sometimes do not work the way we expect. There is one more thing about classroom management: when there are unexpected misconducts, discipline is indeed necessary to ensure the efficiency of teaching and learning activities in language classrooms. Discipline refers to a code of conduct a teacher uses when student behavior is interfering with the operations in the classroom. In a sense, negative student behavior of this type gives the teacher a clear indication that his or her classroom management is proving inadequate. Therefore, discipline is essential and necessary for the teacher as well as the students.

To ensure a disciplined and effective classroom context, the teacher shall hold the following in mind.

1) Know what you want and what you don't want.

2) Show and tell your students what you want.

3) When you get what you want, acknowledge (not praise) it.

4) When you get something else, act quickly and appropriately.

Harmer (1983) and Ur (1996) both suggest some principles to deal with discipline problems. But Ur's suggestions for dealing with undisciplined acts are more detailed than Harmer's. The following are suggestions on discipline in actual teaching practice.

Before the problem arises, a teacher should know how to prevent them from occurring in the first place. Ur (1996) states that the teachers successfully maintaining discipline in class are not those good at dealing with problems, but those who know how to prevent them from occurring in the first place. At this stage, some preventative strategies should be taken.

1) Plan and organize the lesson carefully.

2) Make sure instructions are clear, assertive, brief.

3) Engage the students with tasks.

4) Have eye contact with the class.

5) Keep in touch with what is going on.

When the problem is beginning, it is advisable for the teacher to respond immediately and actively to any incipient problem that is detected. He suggests:

1) Deal with the problem quietly; prevent escalation.

2) Don't take things personally.

3) Rearrange the seats.

4) Change the activity.

5) Don't use threats (unless you are prepared to implement them)!

When the problem has exploded, he suggests the following:

1) "Explode" yourself (with a loud and assertive command).

2) Give in.

3) Make them an offer they can't refuse ( postponement, arbitration, compromise).

4) Talk to the students after class.

5) Stop the class.

6) Use the institution.

## 7.3　Questions for Discussion

> What are the crucial components of an effective lesson plan?
> Will a lesson plan guarantee everything in the classroom? If not,

what is needed in classroom teaching?

➢ What is classroom management? What do you think is important for classroom management?

➢ Go back to 6.1.4 and 6.2.4, work out lesson plans for the cases provided.

# Chapter 8
Teacher Education and Development

*What teachers do in classroom is powerfully affected by the outlooks and orientations of the colleagues with whom they work now and with whom they have worked in the past. In this respect, teacher cultures, the relationships between teachers and their colleagues, are among the most educationally significant aspects of teachers' lives and work. They provide a vital context for teacher development and for the ways that teachers teach. What goes on inside a teacher's classroom cannot be divorced from the relations that are forged outside it.*

(Hargreaves, 1994)

Teacher education and development seems to be more crucial in today's competitive climate and has become the topic in a body of literature (Moulton, 1963; Ur, 1996; Freeman & Richards, 2002; Murray & Christison, 2011; Bartels, 2005). Ur (1996) has made a radical comment that teacher education and development not only makes significant sense for the teachers themselves to achieve a sense of progress and professional advancement, but also makes a crucial difference between survival and dropping out in this career.

Teaching is an art as well as science. To some extent, teaching a language involves language training, observation of class instructions, synthesis of individual experience and others' experiences, reflection on what is going on in teaching and formulation of its principles in instructional practices. A successful teacher should always be ready to keep regular contact with new ideas and their classroom application. As Widdowson (1990) points out, the nature of language teaching, in general, is a principled professional activity in which theory and practice are interdependent upon each other for reciprocal enhancement.

As we have put earlier in Chapter 1, regarding the complexity of all the factors in teaching practice, a teacher can hardly do a better job without resorting to some guiding principles or theories. Contrarily, without retrospection of and meditation on the experiences in real instructional practice, the teacher cannot bring the guiding principles into full play, let alone the gradual accomplishment of them. Widdowson (1990) further points out that teacher education "provides for the appraisal of ideas in order to make them more practically effective, because an understanding of abstract concepts and their relationships allows for adaptability in their realization."

Therefore, teacher education and development sound equally important. Those are what a successful language teacher should have.

Wallace (1991) distinguishes between three models of teacher education: the craft model or the mentoring model, the applied science model or "from theory to practice model" and the reflective model or the inquiry-based model. In the craft model, an inexperienced teacher is paired with a master practitioner who demonstrates to the student-teacher how things should be done. In the applied science model, relevant research findings of scientific knowledge and experimentation are linked with practical teaching. In the reflective model, which was proposed by Wallace, trainees combine received instruction with their own experiential knowledge of the classroom and research; teacher education, and teaching occur concurrently.

Ur's insights into teacher development include personal reflection and interaction with colleagues. He points out that the first and most important basis for professional progress is the reflection on daily classroom events. It is "the necessary basis and jump-off point for further development and the hallmark of the conscientious professional" (Ur, 1996). On the other hand, informal interaction with colleagues will contribute to the development through discussion, and you may find solutions to your problems, get new ideas to your teaching, or confirm your positions.

Wang Qiang (王蔷, 2000) adapted Wallace's reflective model into three stages from which we see the development of professional competence for a language teacher. She seems to combine the craft model, the applied model, and the reflective model. Stage 1 is language training. All language teachers are supposed to have a sound command of the language they teach. Stage 2 involves learning, practice, and reflection. Learning is the preparation that a language teacher should make before going to practice. He or she learns from others' experience, received knowledge, and personal experience. And then, he or she puts them into practice and, at the same time, reflects on what is going on and, in turn, refines practice in teaching. Stage 3 is professional competence. But it is not the ultimate goal, for professional competence can never be finally attained.

Davies & Pearse (2002) suggest three broad categories of teacher development: self-development, cooperative development, and formal development. Self-development involves constant reflection, diary writing about your teaching activities, recording lessons, and reading to keep up with the growth in the profession. Cooperative development consists in sharing with colleagues and peer observation. Formal development includes in-service training programs, which not only improve teachers' teaching skills but also raise teachers' professional status and increase teachers' value in the job market. Formal development programs also include conferences, seminars, and short courses, which offer an opportunity to hear first-hand what is going on in English language teaching worldwide and share your ideas and experiences with other teachers.

It is not difficult to sense that though they define teacher education and development from different angles, there are a lot of similarities in their views. First, language teachers should be well prepared in the field of language teaching, for instance, a good mastery of the language they teach, proper training in teaching skills, integration of language teaching and learning theories and interdisciplinary branches. Second, peer observation and discussion are crucial for language teaching. This shared experience may help you find solutions to your problems, get new ideas to your teaching, confirm your positions or gain a sense of mutual encouragement. Third, reflection is also one of the most important factors for the success of a language teacher. It helps you clarify your ideas and find where you are. Of course, formal training programs, conferences, seminars or short courses are as important as the others.

Professional competence is "a moving target or horizon, towards which professionals travel all their professional life but which is never finally attained" (Wallace, 1991). Nevertheless, on the other hand, as long as we try our best to take advantage of all resources to forward our professional learning, we will get closer to professional competence.

# References

胡壮麟, 姜望琪. 2002. 语言学高级教程. 北京: 北京大学出版社.

李庭芗. 1983. 英语教学法. 北京: 高等教育出版社.

舒白梅. 2005. 现代外语教育学. 上海: 上海外语教育出版社.

束定芳. 2004. 现代外语教学: 理论、实践与方法. 上海: 上海外语教育出版社.

王蔷. 2000. 英语教学法教程. 北京: 高等教育出版社.

王寅. 2005. 认知语言学探索. 重庆: 重庆出版社.

Angelo, A. & Cross, K. 1993. *Classroom Assessment Techniques: A Handbook for College Teachers* (2nd ed.). San Francisco: Jossey-Bass.

Aristotle. 1985. *Nicomachean Ethics.* Terence Irwin, Trans. Indianapolis, IN: Hacket.

Arnold, J. (ed.). 1999. *Affect in Language Learning.* Cambridge: Cambridge University Press.

Asher, J. 1979. *Learning Another Language Through Actions.* San Jose: AccuPrint.

Bach, D. 1977. *Illusions: The Adventures of a Reluctant Messiah.* Bexhill: Gardners Books.

Bartels, N. 2005. *Applied Linguistics and Language Teacher Education.* Boston: Springer.

Bloomfield, L. 1973. *Language.* London: George Allen & Unwin Ltd.

Boers, F. & Lindstromberg, S. 2008. *Cognitive Linguistic Approaches to Teaching Vocabulary and Phraseology.* Berlin/Boston: De Gruyter Mouton.

Brown, G. & Yule, E. 1983. *Discourse Analysis.* Cambridge: Cambridge University Press.

Brownell, J. 1986. *Building Active Listening Skills.* New Jersey: Prentice-Hall.

Bruner, J. 1973. *Going Beyond the Information Given.* New York: Norton.

Bruner, J. 1987. *Actual Minds, Possible Worlds*. Cambridge: Harvard University Press.

Byrne, D. 1988. *Teaching Writing Skills*. In K. Johnson & K. Morrow (eds.). *Communication in the Classroom*. London: Longman.

Cadierno, T. & Eskildsen, W. 2015. *Used-Based Perspectives on Second Language Learning*. Berlin/Boston: De Gruyter Mouton.

Carrell, P. & others. (eds. ) 1988. *Interactive Approaches to Second Language Reading*. Cambridge: Cambridge University Press.

Chomsky, N. 1975. *Reflections on Language*. New York: Pantheon.

Croft, W. & Cruse, D. 2004. *Cognitive Linguistics*. Cambridge: Cambridge University Press.

Curran, A. 1976a. *Counseling-Learning: A Whole-Person Model for Education*. New York: Crune and Stratton.

Curran, A. 1976b. *Counseling-Learning in Second Language*. Apple River, III. : Apple River Press.

Davies, P. & Pearse, E. 2002. *Success in English Teaching*. Shanghai: Shanghai Foreign Language Education Press.

De Knop, S. & De Rycker, T. 2008. *Cognitive Approaches to Pedagogical Grammar: A Volume in Honour of René Dirven*. Berlin/Boston: De Gruyter Mouton.

Dechant, E. 1991. *Understanding and Teaching Reading: An Interactive Model*. Hillsdale, NJ: Lawrence Erlbaum.

Dewey, J. 1997. *Experience and Education*. Florence: Free Press.

Dirven, R., Niemeier, S. & Pütz, R. 2001. "Introduction". In Pütz, M. , Niemeier, S. & Dirven, R. 2001a. *Applied Cognitive Linguistics I: Theory and Language Acquisition*. Berlin/Boston: De Gruyter Mouton.

Dirven, R. & Verspoor, M. 1998. *Cognitive Exploration of Language and Linguistics*. Amsterdam: John Benjamins.

Elliot, J. 1991. *Action Research for Educational Change*. Milton Keynes: Open University Press.

Ellis, R. 1999. *Understanding Second Language Acquisition*. Shanghai: Shanghai Foreign Language Education Press.

Evans, G. & Green, M. 2006. *Cognitive Linguistics: An Introduction*. Edinburgh: Edinburgh University Press.

Foster, P. 1999. "Key Concepts in ELT: Task-Based Learning and Pedagogy". *ELT Journal*, Vol. 53/1.

Freeman, D. 2000. *Techniques and Principles in Language Teaching*. Oxford: Oxford University Press.

Freeman, D. & J. Richards. 2002. *Teacher Learning in Language Teaching*. Shanghai: Shanghai Foreign Language Education Press.

Gattegno, C. 1972. *Teaching Foreign Languages in Schools: The Silent Way*. New York: Educational Solutions.

Geschwind, N. 1979. Specializations of the human brain. *Scientific American*, 192.

Goodman, K. 1967. "Reading, A Psycholinguistic Guess Game". *Journal of the Reading Specialist*, May, 126-135.

Gough, P., Hoover, W. & Peterson, C. 1996. Some observations on a simple view of reading. In C. Cornoldi and J. Oakhill (eds.) *Reading Comprehension Difficulties*. Mahwah, NJ: Lawrence Erlbaum.

Gower, R., Phillips, D. & Walters, S. 1995. *The Teaching Practice Handbook*. Harlow: Longman.

Halliday, M. A. K. 1970. "Language Structure and Language Function". In J. Lyons (ed.) *New Horizons in Linguistics*. Harmondsworth: Penguin.

Hargreaves, A. 1994. *Changing Teachers, Changing Times*. London: Cassell.

Harley, A. 2001. *The Psychology of Language: From Data to Theory*. Hove: Psychology Press.

Harmer, J. 1983. *The Practice of English Language Teaching*. London: Longman.

Harmer, J. 1998. *How to Teach English*. London: Longman.

Hedge, T. 1988. *Writing*. Oxford: Oxford University Press.

Hedge, T. 2002. *Teaching and Learning in the Language Classroom*. Shanghai: Shanghai Foreign Language Education Press.

Holliday, A. 1994. *Appropriate Methodology and Social Context*. Cambridge: Cambridge University Press.

Holme, R. 2009. *Cognitive Linguistics and Language Teaching*. New York: Palgrave Macmillan.

Hopkins, A. & Tribble, C. 1989. *Outlines*. London: Longman.

Joyce, B., Weil, M. & Calhoun, E. 2014. *Models of Teaching*. New York: Pearson.

Kenworthy, J. 1989. *Sounds English: Pronunciation Practice Book & Audio Tape (ELT Skills)*. New York: Pearson Education Ltd.

Kermer, F. 2016. *A Cognitive Grammar Approach to Teaching Tense and Aspect in the L2 Context*. Newcastle: Cambridge Scholars Publishing.

Krashen, S. P. 1981. *Second Language Acquisition and Second Language Learning*. Oxford: Pergamon.

Kress, G. 1985. *Linguistic Process in Sociocultural Practice*. Oxford: Oxford University Press.

Langacker, R. W. 1987. *Foundations of Cognitive Grammar Vol. I: Theoretical Prerequisites*. Stanford: Stanford University Press.

Langacker, R. W. 1991. *Foundations of Cognitive Grammar Vo. II: Descriptive Application*. Stanford: Stanford University Press.

Leech, G. 1974. *Semantics*. Harmondsworth: Penguin.

Lewis, M. 1993. *The Lexical Approach*. Hove: Language Teaching Publications.

Littlemore, J. 2009. *Applying Cognitive Linguistics to Second Language Learning and Teaching*. New York: Palgrave Macmillan.

Long, H. 1975. "Group Work and Communicative Competence in ESOL Classroom". In M. K. Burt and H. C. Dulay (eds. ) *On TESOL 1975: New Directions in Second Language Learning, Teaching, and Bilingual Education*. Washington: TESOL, 210-214.

McCormick, T. 1988. *Theories of Reading in Dialogue: An Interdisciplinary Study*. New York: University Press of America.

McDonough, J. & Shaw, C. 2004. *Materials and Methods in EFT: A Teacher's Guide*. Beijing: Peking University Press.

Moulton, W. 1963. "Linguistics and Language teaching in the United States 1940-1960", *IRAL*, 1 (21): 41.

Mount, H. 2013. "If you don't know grammar, you can't write English". *The Telegraphy*. Retrieved at: http: //blogs. telegraph. co. uk/culture/ harry mount/ 100068896/if-you-don't-know-grammar-you-cant-write-english.

Murray, D. & M. Christison, 2011. *What English Language Teachers Need to Know (Volume I)*. New York: Routledge.

Nunan, D. 1989. *Designing Tasks for the Communicative Classroom*. Cambridge:

Cambridge University Press.

Nunan, D. 2004. *Practical English Language Teaching*. Beijing: Beijing Higher Education Press.

Nuttall, C. 1982. *Teaching Reading Skills in a Foreign Language*. London: Heinemann Educational Books.

Nystrand, M., Doyle, A. & Himley, M. 1986. A critical examination of the doctrine of autonomous texts. In M. Nystrand (ed.), *The Structure of Written Communication*. Orlando, FL: Academic Press.

Payne, V. 1969. *The Lively Art of Writing*. New York: Penguin Books.

Piaget, J. 1972. *The Psychology of the Child*. New York: Basic Books.

Pressley, M. 2000. "What should comprehension instruction be the instruction of?". In Kamil, M. L., Mosenthal, P. B., Pearson, P. D. and Barr, S. R. (eds.) *Handbook of Reading Research*, Vol. 3, 545–561. Mahwah, NJ: Erlbaum.

Pritchard, A. & Woollard, J. 2010. *Psychology for the Classroom: Constructivism and Social Learning*. London & New York: Routledge.

Pütz, M., Niemeier, S. & Dirven, R. 2001a. *Applied Cognitive Linguistics I: Theory and Language Acquisition*. Berlin/Boston: De Gruyter Mouton.

Pütz, M., Niemeier, S. and Dirven, R. 2001b. *Applied Cognitive Linguistics II: Language Pedagogy*. Berlin/Boston: De Gruyter Mouton.

Richards, C. 1990. "The Dilemma of Teacher Education in Second Language Teaching". In C. Richards & D. Nunan (eds.) *Second Language Teacher Education*. Cambridge: Cambridge University Press.

Richards, J. & Rodgers, T. 1986. *Approaches and Methods in Language Teaching*. Cambridge: Cambridge University Press.

Richardson, J., R. Morgan & C. Fleener. 2008. *Reading to Learn in Content Areas*. Belmont: Wadsworth Publishing.

Rivers, W. & Temperley, M. 1978. *A Practical Guide to the Teaching of English*. Oxford: Oxford University Press.

Robinson, P. & Ellis, N. 2008. *Handbook of Cognitive Linguistics and Second Language Acquisition*. New York/London: Routledge.

Ruddell, B. & Speaker, R. 1985. "The interactive reading process: A model. " In Singer and Ruddell. 1985. *Theoretical Models and the Processes of Reading* (3rd eds). Newark, DE: International Reading Association.

Rodgers, T. 2001. *Language Teaching Methodology*. Retrieved July 15, 2006 from the website: http: //www. cal. org/ericcll/digest/rodgers. html.

Rumelhart, E. 1985. "Toward an interactive model of reading. " In Singer and Ruddell 1985. *Theoretical Models and the Processes of Reading*. 3rd edition. Newark, DE: International Reading Association.

Sinclair, J. & Coulthard, M. 1975. *Towards an Analysis of Discourse*. Oxford: Oxford University Press.

Smith, N. 1999. *Chomsky: Ideas and Ideals*. Cambridge: Cambridge University Press.

Sperber, D. & Wilson, D. 2004. *Relevance: Communication and Cognition* (2nd eds.). Oxford: Blackwell Publishing.

Stern, H. 1983. *Fundamental Concepts of Language Teaching*. Oxford: Oxford University Press.

Taylor, J. 2003. *Cognitive Grammar*. Oxford: Oxford University Press.

Thorndike, E. 1932. *The Fundamentals of Learning*. New York: Teachers College Press.

Tolstoy, L. 1903. *Pedagogical Writings*. Moscow: Kushnerev.

Tomasello, M. 2003. *Constructing a Language: A Usage-based Theory of Language Acquisition*. Cambridge, MA: Harvard University Press.

Tribble, C. 1996. *Writing*. Oxford: Oxford University Press.

Tyler, R. 1949. *Basic Principles of Curriculum and Instruction*. Chicago: University of Chicago Press.

Ur, P. 1996. *A Course in Language Teaching: Practice and Theory*. Cambridge: Cambridge University Press.

Vacca, R. & Vacca, J. 1989. *Content Area Reading*. Longman: Longman Higher Education.

Vandergrift, L. 1999. "Facilitating Second Language Listening Comprehension: Acquiring Successful Strategies." *ELT Journal* 53/3, 167-78.

Vygotsky, L. 1978. *Mind in Society*. Cambridge, MA: MIT Press.

Vygotsky, L. 1986. *Thought and Language*. Cambridge, MA: MIT Press.

Wallace, J. 1991. *Training Foreign Languages Teachers*. Cambridge: Cambridge University Press.

Wertheimer, M. 1923. Laws of organization in perceptual forms. In *A Source Book of Gestalt Psychology* (p.71-88). London: Routledge & Kegan Paul.

White, V. & Arndt, V. 1991. *Process Writing*. London: Longman.

Widdowson, G. 1978. *Teaching Language as Communication*. Oxford: Oxford University Press.

Widdowson, H. 1990. *Aspects of Language Teaching*. Oxford: Oxford University Press.

Williams, E. 1984. *Reading in the Language Classroom*. London: Macmillan.

Willis, J. 1996. *A Framework for Task-Based Learning*. Harlow: Longman.

Wright, T. 2005. *Classroom Management in Language Education*. Palgrave: Macmillan.